Life Interrupted

Navigating the Unexpected

PRISCILLA **SHIRER**

B&H
PUBLISHING GROUP

NASHVILLE, TENNESSEE

978-1-4336-7045-9

Published by B&H Publishing Group
Nashville, Tennessee

Dewey Decimal Classification: 248.843
Subject Heading: CHRISTIAN LIFE \ JONAH, PROPHET \
GOD—WILL

5 6 7 8 9 10 • 20 19 18 17 16

For Jude

Acknowledgments

Jerry, I'm in awe of you. Your patience, kindness, care, and concern for the kids and me is stunning. I'm honored to be your wife and your partner in ministry. Thank you for marrying me.

Jackson, Jerry Jr., and Jude. I'm so grateful to be your mom. You are my greatest treasures and my life's best work.

Dad and Mom, thank you for investing in me. I'm hoping that you're feeling rich from the dividends.

Linnae, Carla, and Rachel, thanks for working alongside Jerry and me at GB Ministries. You keep the wheels turning.

Jennifer and the B&H Publishing Team, it's a pleasure to work with you. We consider you to be our family and look forward to doing it again soon.

Lawrence, all I can say is thank you. There'd be a lot of confused readers if it weren't for you!

Contents

Part 1: Interruptions, Interruptions
Chapter 1. And Now for Something Completely Different   1
Chapter 2. Consider It a Privilege   15
Chapter 3. Story of Your Life   32

Part 2: On the Run
Chapter 4. Beyond a Reasonable Doubt   46
Chapter 5. Slippery Slope   59
Chapter 6. Wake-Up Call   72

Part 3: Repentance at Sea
Chapter 7. Now What?   84
Chapter 8. A Fish Called Grace   95
Chapter 9. Making Change   110

Part 4: Second Chances
Chapter 10. There's More Where These Came From   126
Chapter 11. Rinse and Repeat   137
Chapter 12. Go to Ninevah   152

Part 5: Unfinished Business
Chapter 13. God on Our Own Terms   170
Chapter 14. The Many Moods of Jonah   186
Chapter 15. There's So Much More to Tell   198

Notes   213

Part 1

Interruptions, Interruptions

CHAPTER 1

And Now for Something Completely Different

For since the world began, no ear has heard, and no eye has
seen a God like you, who works for those who wait for him!
ISAIAH **64:4** NLT

I wish I'd known then what I know now—what the Lord is helping me begin to discover.

Maybe then, when those unexpected circumstances surprised me, I would've been better able to corral my untamed, unruly emotions.

Maybe then the twists of life wouldn't have caused such a twist in my heart, making me so severe and unforgiving.

Maybe then I would've recognized God's unseen hand in all of it and would've met the frustration or disappointment with a wink and a smirk, knowing He was behind it all, that this interruption was merely His way of laying a foundation for better things.

Maybe then I wouldn't have tried so hard to control it or hurry through it but would've yielded to it and embraced what the Lord allowed.

Maybe.

Maybe not.

But certainly not at the time.

You see, my life was going to be music. Literally. The first time I sang in church, I was five years old. I've got concrete memories of my little wobbly voice and knees that carried me through that day. From that moment on I was sure God wanted me to be a singer. I planned for it, aspired to it, and dreamed of what it would be like to stand on the stage and in the recording studio, singing my songs for Him. I even auditioned for several nationally known singing groups in my late teens and early twenties and was thrilled when they said they'd actually like me to come on board with them.

But people I went to for counsel encouraged me not to jump into music too soon and pass up some other experiences that might prove more valuable later. By the time I'd waited for all the obstacles to clear, those great music opportunities had passed me by. I'd missed my chance. The exciting, open doors that had been accessible to me before were now closed. I was devastated. What was I supposed to do now, when the one thing I'd wanted—the path I thought was God's plan for me—was no longer an available option?

I wish I'd known then what I know now.

Music was apparently out, much to the dismay of my hopes and dreams. So after batting around some alternatives, I decided to pursue a degree in radio and television. It seemed to suit me. If I couldn't do the music thing, I could at least enjoy a stage presence on camera. Television proved to be an intense, high-pressure undertaking—a lot of hard work—but very exciting, especially when some jobs opened up for me at several different stations, performing in various on-air capacities. With each new assignment I truly believed this might be the platform that would elevate me to bigger and better things. But each time I started working for a particular show, their ratings began to suffer. Every single one was cancelled within a year of my joining the team. (Talk about giving a girl a complex!)

This couldn't be happening. I had studied for this. I had put in the hours. I was paying my dues and was absolutely certain the Lord had steered me toward doing this for a career, for a livelihood. Obviously, then, I had either heard Him wrong, or He had set me up to fail. What does a singer and broadcast professional do when nothing she feels called to is working out? I was barely in my twenties. And already feeling washed up.

I wish I'd known then what I know now.

Meanwhile, I was dating a young man, a wonderful guy who had captured my heart and seemed like the one I wanted to spend the rest of my life with. We had gotten pretty serious, even beginning to make those first, sunny promises of marriage. But in one of those twists and turns on the road to romantic bliss, our car had run off the road. We were done. And I was totally distressed. I begged God to restore my relationship with this man. We were meant to be together. I knew it! But despite all the talks and times spent together, all the plans and dreams we had begun imagining—fact was, he didn't want me anymore. And it came close to killing me. I couldn't sleep. I couldn't eat. I couldn't see anything good in store for me. I was losing at life and losing at love, all at the same time.

I wish I'd known then what I know now.

There *was* somebody else for me. Years later I was in love. (More on that later.) And after three years of marriage, with little effort, God allowed me to get pregnant. We were thrilled. Soon, however, almost before the reality of "baby makes three" had even begun to hit us, I miscarried. Where we had hardly been able to keep our minds on anything else because of our excited anticipation, now we could hardly keep our minds on anything else because of our grief and disappointment.

Life. Interrupted again.

How could this happen? Why would God allow it? Did it mean we'd *never* be able to have children? Could we possibly get past this horrible experience and dare to try again, knowing how low the lows can be when your joy is snatched away?

Yes, we could.

Yes, we did.

First came Jackson. Then two years later, Jerry Jr. And when these fun little guys began rounding the corner from toddlerhood to the school-age years, Jerry and I decided we were closing up shop in the baby-making business. We both loved being parents but were so looking forward to life without diapers, sippy cups, and colicky crying spells in the middle of the night. I was fairly certain I didn't have another pregnancy/baby/toddler experience in me.

Well . . . yes, I did.

When those faint pink lines shaded their way into a plus-sign on the pregnancy test I'd brought home from the store, Jerry's and my plan for a new phase of life suddenly became our plan for an unexpected phase of life. This was not what we had in mind. We had felt so complete and satisfied with our two little boys and our nice little life, and—dare I say it—we were *shocked* to realize we were now headed in another direction: a six-pound, twelve-ounce change of plans by the name of Jude Maddox Shirer. And as sweet and good-natured fellow as he is, the October he was born represented a whole new chapter in our household—an unexpected one.

Then in the midst of trying to adjust my emotions and plans to suit this new development, our stable, settled ministry began to experience some growing pains of its own. While my pregnant waistline was expanding with no regard for the contents in my closet, our ministry seemed to be following suit. With a growing family to manage and a full load of ministry responsibilities to contend with already—even before having to think about adding a new baby to the mix—we were stunned to be thrust into another realm of opportunity and challenge. Our tiny staff (of which my husband and I made up two-thirds) was already stretched to the limit. We were grateful and excited, of course, about what we saw God doing. It's just that we were caught a bit off guard. We'd been content with the regular pace of family and ministry life as we'd known it for several years. We had learned how to find our rhythm and balance, but now things were changing. *Everything* was changing. Personally and professionally.

So a lot of things had happened along the way to alter my planned trajectory of life. A music ministry? Maybe not. Television career? Maybe not. That first expectation of marriage? First baby? Maybe not. Two parents, two kids—let's call it a completed family? Umm, maybe not. *Lord, how about at least an easily managed ministry?* Certainly not.

I wish I knew then what I'm starting to see now.

Call it the interrupted life.

—— You Want Me to What? ——

I suspect that you, too, have experienced some interruptions along the way. It may have been something tragic—the death of someone close to you, a health scare, a debilitating accident. A love lost. An opportunity missed. A life goal unreached. It may have caused such a drastic change in your moods and makeup and manner of living, you almost don't remember who you were before it happened. In many ways you've become defined by this thing that occurred, this one startling event that threw everything off balance.

But interruptions are not limited to huge, horrible things. In fact, they can be rather minor by comparison. Car trouble. Chicken pox. A funny, spoiled smell in the meat you'd set out to cook for dinner. Still, it's caught you by surprise. You weren't expecting it. You were traveling along with your list of to-dos in mind, fully knowing what the day held when something just crept up out of nowhere and caught you off guard. Suddenly your schedule is shot to pieces, along with all your preset notions on what it would take to get everything done. You've been blindsided, forced to deal with a new wrinkle, a new obstacle to navigate around.

Interruptions.

They come in all sizes. Large and small. Anywhere between majorly challenging and mildly inconvenient. An unforeseen hit to your family budget. A best friend moving out of town. A spouse confessing that he hasn't been totally honest with you about something. A doctor's report that is less than desirable. A pregnancy test that reads negative . . . again. A new supervisor at work who's nothing like the last one you'd grown to like so much. Another year of singleness when marriage is what you want. A sister who's going in for surgery and needs you to watch her kids for a few days.

It may even be something good. Like being asked to take on a new role in ministry, or finding out you have *three* babies in that belly of yours instead of just one. (Yes, that happened to a friend of mine.) Helping your daughter plan a summer wedding, or having to move to another state to accommodate a promotion. But even these good interruptions are going to take a lot of your time. They're going to make things different than you've been accustomed to. They're going to cost you an expense you hadn't accounted for right now. So how do you respond? What's the best way to navigate the unexpected—a *Life Interrupted*?

Just to be clear: I *hate* interruptions! While I'm a spontaneous girl who enjoys impromptu adventures and activities on occasion, whenever I get a goal or plan fixed in my mind, I'm as persistent as the little squirrel I watched scouting for acorns in my backyard this morning. I don't want to be detoured until that nut is in my paws, in my mouth, then . . . mmm . . . in my tummy. Any detour away from that mission makes me antsy and unsettled. It's the way I've always been. Stick-to-itiveness, I think they call it. A good, healthy trait but—watch out—one that can quickly morph into one of my worst when I'm not willing to bend and flex to God's will, when I'm pretty sure what He wants is different from my aspiration.

That's what I found myself facing when little Jude was on the way and I was trying desperately to figure out how I'd be able to balance the demands of a growing family and ministry. I loved my life but felt stretched to the limit. So I knew my heart wasn't exactly into this. Didn't God know that Jerry and I had spent lots of time carefully crafting these plans for our lives? We'd given away all the baby paraphernalia in our certainty that our family was complete. The crib was gone. The baby swing was gone. The bouncy seat was gone, and lo and behold, I had some semblance of a waistline for the first time in years. Both of our kids had graduated out of toddlerhood, and I had mentally refocused myself onto a life with two young boys who (unlike when they were babies) could verbalize to me where it hurt, what was wrong, and how I could help.

So, again, I admit I was whining a little bit. Complaining. Those first few months of morning sickness were, uh—let's just say, I was not the kind of Priscilla you'd want to be around. It was not my best moment, I assure you, especially as our ministry was growing and we knew we'd need to add to our staff if we wanted any chance of keeping up. We liked it small and intimate the way it was, but it couldn't stay that way any longer. Obviously, both of these things (the new baby and the growth in ministry) were gifts from God, but let's be honest—sometimes God's gifts are disguised beneath new responsibilities.

One day in the midst of my self-imposed pity party, I got the feeling God was asking me a question. Was I going to be a whiner, a complainer, a grumbler, a martyr, someone who wanted everybody to feel sorry for her the rest of her life even when there was really nothing to feel sorry for me about? Was this going to become my pattern for how I handled things that didn't go my way? Was this the kind of person my husband and family would need to get used to living with?

Or was I going to yield to what God was calling me to do—not just physically with this pregnancy and the additional needs in ministry but also in my attitude, my mind, my heart, my spirit? Was I going to surrender myself completely to Him? Was I going to embrace His plans for me?

Turns out God was about to send me *another* blessed interruption.

Not just Jude, my new little son, but Jonah.

In the pages of Jonah's well-known book of the Bible, God began to speak a new word to my heart. Even as I was wrestling with my interrupted life, God started showing me some things through the eyes of a runaway prophet, a man who *also* was interrupted from a life of relative comfort. A man who saw God's change of plans as something to be avoided and escaped at all costs. A man who would eventually need a raging sea storm and three days in a fish's belly before he would come to terms with what surrender was all about and what it could accomplish.

I didn't want to be like Jonah. I didn't want to require God to reach into His bottom drawer of disciplinary tactics before I came around to His way of thinking. As much as I may not have planned to take on the responsibility of a newborn baby again—not right at that moment, at least—or felt we were prepared to take on the new responsibilities that ministry growth would undoubtedly require, I *really* didn't want the responsibility of becoming a person who thinks she knows more than God does. I've seen that in myself before. I saw it in Jonah again. And I did not want to be that kind of woman anymore.

Honestly, knowing my track record with God and how He's shown Himself strong in the face of all my life interruptions, I should've handled this phase of my life differently. I was a bit disappointed in myself. Because looking back, I had a lot to thank God for. You see, if I had joined one of those singing groups in my teenage years, putting my life on hold while chasing a dream God knew wasn't for me, I would've probably continued on that path long after I'd forgotten that my first job in life was not to sing for the Lord but to listen for His direction and guidance. I'm pretty sure now that His plan for me all along was to be involved in teaching ministry. And I'm just as sure that if I'd been out on the singing circuit, I would've made the journey back a much longer road than it was supposed to be. In fact, I might never have gotten here at all.

If only I'd known.

Those years I spent studying television and getting some great on-air experience seemed largely wasted to me at one time. But what I once considered a pointless detour turned out to be the ideal training ground for the video-driven Bible studies God knew I'd be involved in later on.

If only I could've seen it, could've trusted Him.

And what if that relationship—the one I'd wanted to become my marriage—had not been interrupted like it was? Looking back at it now, I can see God's hand involved in turning me away from one man and turning my heart toward another. It takes a certain kind of guy to handle the life that our marriage and ministry require. Had the first man decided to marry me—who knows, we might have been happy together, but I'm sure now that he wasn't the one I really needed. He wasn't tailored for me like Jerry is, ideal for what God knew would be required of a husband in a situation like ours. Apart from accepting Christ as my Savior, Jerry is the best decision I've ever made (or better yet, like my seven-year-old said to me the other night, "Daddy's the best decision God ever made for you.") But I'm telling you, it was hard at the time. I didn't want any piece of God's will that didn't include this other man in it. And yet the wounds he'd left behind made me appreciate all the more the healing salve of Jerry's perfectly suited kindness and love for me. I fell head over heels into the romance of a lifetime. How I thank the Lord now for unanswered prayers. Interruptions are often His way of doing something even better.

I wish I'd known that earlier.

Perhaps Jonah might've wished that, too. He was a prophet to the northern kingdom of Israel during the early part of the eighth century BC. And while we don't know much about his life prior to the events recorded in the book that bears his name, we do know from 2 Kings 14:25 that he had foretold some positive developments for his people, the Hebrews.

During the reign of King Jeroboam II, the nation witnessed a restoration of territories that had been taken by Syria. This allowed Israel to achieve its most prosperous era since Solomon, primarily by allowing them to control most of the important trade routes that ran through Palestine, connecting the far reaches of the ancient world. And Jonah was the prophet who had seen this coming. He had heard from the Lord, declared the details, and been proven right when these welcome events came to fruition. Most likely, therefore, he was popular, highly respected, and greatly appreciated in his role. Handsomely paid, as well, for the stature he enjoyed.

He was living a prophet's dream. And he was more than content for things to keep on going the way they'd always gone, the way he had planned and fully expected they would. He was living for God, doing His work, and doing it well. Why would God ever send him to do something else?

If only he'd known.

And yet Jonah, great prophet that he was, couldn't see any more clearly than we usually can when we try to understand why God would be causing or allowing this interruption to happen to us right now, when the only thing it's doing is making us feel frustrated and put out. It's the last thing we want or seem to need. And yet God has let it happen anyway.

So I could relate to Jonah as I sat there pregnant with our unexpected third son and with new required tasks in our ministry, reading again a story so familiar yet one that God was opening to my eyes in a fresh, new way as I pondered what to do with my resistant heart and its stubborn streak. I knew how it felt, as Jonah did, to experience a clear word from God and want to run in the opposite direction. I knew what it was like to watch circumstances maneuvering around me in such a way that God's hand was obviously on them, drawing me to come along, asking me to trust Him enough to cooperate with His purposes.

But I also knew the desire to rebel. I knew what goes through a person's mind who is not wanting to engage fully in the season of life God is calling her into.

Running from God. Fighting against God's clear will. Jonah certainly did it. In fact, he was the only prophet in the whole Bible who *ever* did it. It's always been easy to judge him or look down on him—one of the bad boys of the Old Testament. Well, it's not that simple for me. Looking down is hard to do when you're so near the bottom yourself, when emotionally you've got one foot out the door and one hand on the steering wheel. Was I going to let my interruptions do to me what Jonah let his do to him?

— What'll It Be Next? —

That's the dilemma that brought me here. To this book. To you, wherever you happen to be. Very personal stuff. Very real life. Just like yours. I know we can relate to what each other is dealing with. I know we share a common language when it comes to understanding what interruptions look like, feel like, sound like, scare us like, bug us like. We've all had our lives altered and redirected along the way. We've all seen our Plan A's take a backseat to other realities—realities we just don't want to accept or live through. Yet here they are. This is our life. We can run, but we can't hide.

Knowing what we know about God, we do our best to accept the fact that we wouldn't be having to put up with this stuff right now if He didn't want us to, if He wasn't allowing it to happen for some reason. But that doesn't always make it a whole lot easier to handle, does it? I may feel upbeat enough to follow along on *some* days, but on others I'm ready to head for the hills or perhaps just sit down and give up.

We've all been Jonah before, haven't we? We've gotten irritated. We've wanted to duck out. We've wished God would go pick on someone else for a change. So something important is still missing inside. Something is keeping us from living out what we say we believe about Him—that we can trust Him even when we don't understand, that He won't lead us astray, that His will is more important than ours.

Why do we still run from Him and His plans?

Well, I was hoping maybe we could learn together, the same way I learned when God sat me down with Jonah, when I looked up from the middle of my *Life Interrupted* and saw some things I wished I'd known a long time ago. I'm not all the way there yet, you understand. But I know I don't want to let one more interruption send me off frantically dodging God's will and missing out on what He's wanting to accomplish in me and through me. I want my life to radiate what happens when God has a person's heart at His full control, when every event or circumstance is simply another avenue to know Him better and show forth His glory.

That's what the book of Jonah is really all about. It's not just about the big fish—not just Jonah and "the whale." The main character in Jonah's story is God. Every single chapter—in fact, every single verse—speaks of the grandeur of God, the grace of God, the sovereignty of God, the beckoning of God, the discipline of God. Everywhere you look in this tiny piece of ancient historical literature, God is there. He's *always* there. He is right in the middle of every interruption.

So if you're feeling the pinch of the interrupted life, guess what? God is right here in the middle of yours too, even if it's something you've sort of brought on yourself (as many of mine have been). This interruption—whatever it is, no matter how big or small—represents your next best chance to see Him take center stage, to show you what He can do when the unexpected only makes you more expectant than ever.

Like you I've run from change. I've run from life's surprises. Sometimes I've run just to keep moving when I didn't know what else to do. But I've run into a problem. Because in running toward what I thought was better, safer, more pleasurable, more fulfilling, less painful, less complicated, or less confining, I've actually been running from God, from His will, and from His blessing.

And I'm tired of running. Aren't you?

What if we *knew* this interrupted life was less about the problem and more about the process? What if we *knew* this roadblock or aggravation hadn't caught God by surprise even if it's come as a shock to us? What if we *knew* that the direction He was taking us provided opportunities we'd always dreamed about, even if they didn't look exactly the way we thought they would? What if we *knew*, by not getting what we want, God was ultimately giving us something better?

I think we can know—and *live* like we know.

And Jonah's place is a good place to go to find out how.

CHAPTER 2

Consider It a Privilege

The word of the LORD came to Jonah the son of Amittai saying . . .

JONAH 1:1

I was a proud member of the junior high girls' volleyball team at Brook Hollow Christian School near Dallas, Texas. I say "proud" because even though the conservative code of our school meant we were prohibited from wearing the customary short shorts other teams wore, we had something nobody else had: culottes. Red, ankle-length culottes. Emphasis on the "cool."

It sounds funny to say it now, but we really did think we were stylin' at the time. Crisp, white jerseys with red numbers and red trim. We looked so sharp in our uniforms that when we lined up in game formation, there was no doubt in our minds that the other team was totally intimidated. One step on the court, and they had to know we meant business.

Just one problem with our volleyball team. We couldn't play volleyball.

We'd see that white leather Wilson volleyball sailing over the net in our direction, and three or four of us would call out, "I got it! I got it!" But everybody yelling all at once like that would scare us into thinking somebody else really did have it. So we'd each back off and just be standing there as the ball thudded to the floor between us. Another point for another winning opponent. We may have *thought* we had it, but the truth was—nobody had it.

We Christians are a lot like that today. We look so good. We've got all the right gear on. We sway to the worship music. We know how to wave the holy hand. We've got Bibles and Christian books all over the house. We drive off to church on Sundays with our outfits pressed and our hair done. We look good. We've got it.

Then God sends His will for us sailing into our court. A new personal mission or challenge. An interruption to our well-coordinated routine. Maybe it's a child diagnosed with a health issue or special need. Maybe it's an aging parent needing regular drives to the doctor's office or tough decisions made concerning their round-the-clock care. Maybe it's an added work assignment, dropped in your lap because of the company's latest decision to do more with less. We see it looming closer, like a volleyball arcing over the net at us. Growing larger and harder to avoid all the time.

Suddenly, instead of feeling so confident and put together, so incredibly Christian, we point to somebody else and say, "You get it."

We don't want it.

And yet when you and I signed up as followers of Christ, we all said to the Lord that we would do anything He told us to do. "Not my will, but Yours be done." In just about any worship service we happen to be attending, on any given week we so enjoy singing His praises, declaring ourselves gratefully available to Him for whatever He wants of us, whenever He wants it. But then through the week, He starts revealing what His will is actually going to be for us moment by moment, day by day, decision by decision. He lobs a shot onto our side of the court, something we don't feel ready for or interested in handling, and we say, "Hold on, Lord, I didn't mean I'd do that!"

It's what we call an interruption. And we hate it.

God was calling Jonah to go to Nineveh. And Jonah hated Nineveh. Like perhaps the way someone hates thinking about that person who abused them, or that spouse who left them, or that offender who attacked them. He hated *Nineveh*, and *Ninevites*, and everything Nineveh stood for. Their brutality toward his people—their cruel methods and reputation—made him physically sick to hear God even mention their name, much less be ordered to go there and interact with them.

So I wonder if Jonah felt like it was going to be a privilege doing business with God on this.

I'm fairly certain he didn't. Why? Because I am Jonah. And I know I have a hard time considering any interruption to my established plans a *privilege*, no matter how small or short-lived it happens to be, especially if He's directing me toward someone or something I don't particularly like. Yes, I want to serve God—as long as it's convenient. Yes, I want to do His will—until it becomes a tad uncomfortable for me. Yes, I want to hear His Word—as long as it's more about *telling* people things than actually having to do things, as long as He's not asking me to get more involved than I already am, as long as it doesn't mean I have to deviate much from the way I've been operating thus far. As long as I like it.

So when "the word of the LORD came to Jonah the son of Amittai saying, 'Arise, go to Nineveh the great city and cry against it, for their wickedness has come up before Me'" (Jon. 1:1–2), it doesn't take a big fish slapping me in the head to imagine what went through Jonah's mind. This was not what he wanted to do.

This was not where he wanted to go. He did not think it was nice of God to lay this kind of errand on someone who was already plenty busy doing important things for Him right here at home.

- *Nineveh.* It's something to which God calls you or permits into your life that is not in your plans, somewhere He redirects you that is off the well-designed path you were aiming to follow.
- *Nineveh.* It's the serious health problem He's allowed you to face, and you know He's not only calling you to endure it physically but also to be a light of faith and Christian hope to every doctor and nurse tech and fellow patient you come across, whether you feel like it or not.
- *Nineveh.* It's seeing the economy do a number on your nest egg just as you're reaching retirement age, meaning God is expecting you not only to do more with less but also to do it with a heart that trusts Him—happily, thankfully—regardless of what your checkbook balance shows.
- *Nineveh.* It's the season of singleness that's persisted into your thirties or forties despite the many years of praying for a godly spouse, and now He's clearly showing you that the person you thought might be the one is obviously not.
- *Nineveh.* It's that certain period of life you're not happy about entering, that feeling of watching your own plans become derailed while an unexpected and likely less desirable plan begins taking shape around you.

Don't you just hate it when that happens?

Interruptions mean upheaval, revised agendas, frustration over not being able to do what we want to do. The dictionary describes it with such words as "to thwart" and "to hinder" and "to break uniformity." Interruptions always seem bad. Who wouldn't want to avoid one by any means possible if they could? They're trouble. They cause nothing but problems. That's why the word *interruption* has such a negative connotation, right?

But interruptions are only negative when we deem the person, problem, or circumstance that's forcing itself on us to be of less value or interest than what we were doing before. It's like hearing the phone ring while you're walking out the door or stepping into the shower. If it's a telemarketer who doesn't understand why you're not interested in adding something like *twenty-five hundred channels* to your cable package, it's a rude interruption. It's just putting you five minutes further behind than you already were. But if it's a couple from church, telling you that God has placed a burden on their heart to give you *$2,500* for a need of yours, it's not an interruption at all.

Same phone. Same time. Much different feeling. It's an issue of value.

We can draw it up this way:

Insignificant Person + Insignificant Task = Interruption

If the person trying to drag you away from your present activity feels relatively unimportant to you, or perhaps just a slight bit annoying, and the task he's wanting you to perform or consider seems undesirable by comparison, you immediately tag it as an interruption, a bother. But if what's beckoning you away seems more compelling to you than what it's keeping you from, then you don't argue with it or even just tolerate it with great reluctance. You choose it. You don't want to miss where it might lead.

And since the Person who really calls the shots in our lives is God, and therefore any task He is assigning to us represents His will for this season of time—meaning, it's the absolute best thing we could be doing at this particular moment!—then we need to change our definition of interruption when it comes to His leading in our lives.

Significant Person + Significant Task =
Divine Intervention

Sure, your plan was great. The course you'd mapped out was admirable. But there's no telling how unimaginably fantastic the destination is that He's trying to get you to follow Him toward.

Now let me pause here to say something important. By changing our terminology to call this a "divine intervention," I'm not saying God has necessarily caused it to happen. If your mate has left you and filed for divorce, this is obviously not what the Lord intended for your marriage. But be sure of this: God has seen it and known about it. He has allowed this stabbing pain to enter your life for some reason known only to His holy providence. And though you cannot understand it or make any sense of why this is occurring, you're being asked whether or not you will trust God even in the midst of this lousy set of circumstances and surrender to what He has allowed. You kinda know what'll happen if you don't. Wonder what might happen if you just . . . do.

Perhaps your husband's work is such that the possibility of relocating every few years is more likely than not. If you only choose to view this as an interruption, you'll grow paralyzed with frustration. But if you see it as a divine intervention, then your eyes will be opened to the new opportunities open to you with each move.

Perhaps the makeup of your predominantly single-race neighborhood and part of town has begun changing to include more immigrants and nationalities. If you and your church despise this interruption to your settled routines and expectations, you'll no doubt miss out on reaching the people whom God has sent you to. But if you see it as a divine intervention, then you'll most likely realize the grand scope of God's will for your ministry that included much more than you originally thought.

Perhaps you only have to deal with your troubled in-laws on the rarest of occasions, but they've mentioned they'd like to come spend Thanksgiving with you this year. If you can't get over being steamed at this interruption to your plans, you'll spend your entire holiday wishing you were somewhere else. But if you see it as a divine intervention, . . . well, you may still wish you were somewhere else, but at least you could become aware of the underlying opportunity God is giving you on this "festive" occasion.

Your response at moments like these indicates whether or not you're going "all in" with God—whether you're going to yield to Him completely or take off like Jonah in another direction of your own choosing, ending up in an even worse place than you're in now.

If you find yourself balking at what God is asking of you today—a new responsibility, an added burden, a frightening unknown, an uncomfortable conversation to be had—it's an indication of the importance you place on Him and His will. It's easy to say that His plans are your most essential endeavors. It's entirely another thing to live like it, to participate with Him even when what He's inviting you to do is something you don't understand and may never have chosen.

One person's interruption is another's divine intervention. One person's problem is another person's privilege.

Which kind of person do you want to be?

— A Divine What? —

I saw a morning news feature recently, one in a series on the religions of the world. The correspondent was filming this particular piece from Hong Kong, standing amid a mountainside shrine containing an enormous, bronze statue of Buddha. She said that in order for her and the camera crew to get into position for their shoot, they had to climb more than a hundred stairs, just as all pilgrims must do if they want to approach this place of prayer. They must climb up to go looking for their god, looking for their sense of purpose and enlightenment, looking for why they matter in the world. Buddha is not coming down to them.

Well, our God—the one true God—is seated on a throne, all right. High and lifted up, living and reigning over all. But this God of ours is willing to come down. I can hardly believe it. He gives us the startling, breathtaking *privilege* of knowing that He desires a relationship with us, entering into our troubled circumstances and leading us deeper into Himself, giving us a divine directive that enables us to participate with Him in His eternal plans, even in the laboratory of our own individual lives. Yes, His intervention may seem frustrating at the moment. It may feel boring, or frightening, or nervous, or awkward, or embarrassing, or even painful. But if we know—I mean, really know that we serve a good, caring, *divinely intervening* God who is "righteous in all His ways and kind in all His deeds" (Ps. 145:17)—we can see more than just a problem. We can see a privilege.

That's why, when we read that "the word of the LORD came to Jonah," we're witnessing an absolute miracle in action. The fact that God would speak to a man in the midst of a crowd of millions and allow Jonah to hear Him is astounding all on its own. When the God of the universe allows a mere human to be included in what He is doing, that person is in an unbelievably privileged position, wouldn't you think? Oh, sure, He could leave us to our own devices, to our meager human arrangements and strategies, but He chooses instead to give us the chance to get in on His. It's easy to forget that God's desire to have a relationship with us is no less wonderful and amazing simply because it's taught on day one in the new members' class. It's still a miracle. It always is.

It is a privilege for you and me as believers in Jesus Christ to hear the voice of God, to sense the stirring of His Holy Spirit—a privilege not everyone gets, only the adopted children of their heavenly Father. It is a privilege for us to look at circumstances and discern God's involvement in them. To recognize them as more than mere happenstance but rather God's own detailed design and plan. To see that He is allowing us to cooperate with Him in bringing life from death, growth from loss, testimony from tragedy.

When He lifts the veil from your eyes in this way so that you begin to recognize His hand in it all, you'll see that He is not interrupting your life to kill your joy. The "word of the Lord" is designed to reshape your purposes, putting you in a position for Him to do through you what you cannot do on your own.

And, of course, like Jonah, we can be opinionated. We can possess very strong attitudes about what God has asked us to do. But often the greatest miracle God can perform for you is right in your own heart. The Bible says to "delight yourself in the LORD; and He will give you the desires of your heart" (Ps. 37:4). This doesn't mean we'll always get what we want or be placed in positions that naturally appeal to us. But if our chief desire is to hear the "word of the LORD"—regardless of what that "word" happens to be—He has promised to change our value judgments until we only want what He wants, until we're totally convinced that anything He would lead us to do or allow us to endure is of more importance than what we were doing before. He will actually give us brand spanking new desires! We'll look up one day and be completely shocked to find ourselves face-to-face with the one thing we thought we'd never want and realize it's not so bad after all.

If we refuse to defer to Him in this way, we'll spend a huge chunk of our remaining years being mad at others, mad at ourselves, even mad at God for not letting us accomplish what we set out to do. No, you may not be having the most fun you've ever had right now, but leave room for the "word of the Lord" to come to you. Hold your own plans loosely and stay ready to submit to His. Consider them to be more important, more desirable than anything you could dream up on your own. He has come down to you with intentionality and purpose because He loves you and knows that you are never more secure than when you're in His will.

Don't look now, but your interruption just became a divine intervention.

—— Nineveh or Bust ——

During the first half of the eighth century BC, when Jonah lived, Nineveh was one of the principle provinces in Assyria. The Assyrians had a reputation for physical and psychological terror, which they freely inflicted on their enemies, not the least of which was Israel. One commentator writes, "It is reasonable to suppose that on one of these expeditions to Israel the Assyrians had laid siege to Gath-Hepher, the hometown of Jonah. Perhaps the city was destroyed and some of its inhabitants slain. Some loved one of Jonah may have suffered and been killed at this time. There is a possibility that his own mother and father were slain before his eyes when he was a boy."[1]

I'll never forget a Rwandan couple coming forward for prayer in our church many years ago. They had been evacuated with other survivors during a spate of murders in their country. And tragically in their rush to safety, they had been forced to leave behind their own children, not knowing if they were alive or dead or if they'd ever see them again. The pain in that mother's eyes. The tears falling down that father's face. I'll never forget it.

Now while the details of how Jonah was personally affected by these tortures at the hands of the Assyrians are purely speculative, we know for sure that Israel as a whole had been brutalized by them, making the mere mention of the name "Nineveh" a source of raw bitterness, dread, and fear for any Israelite—Jonah included. Yet here's where God was calling him to go—to Nineveh—to leave behind his beloved countrymen, his comfort zone, his chief desire in life, and to preach the word of the Lord to his declared enemies.

At this particular point in history, Assyria was experiencing a period of national weakness. And nothing would have thrilled a guy like Jonah more than seeing their momentary decline become their complete demise. The last thing he ever expected, and certainly the last thing he ever wanted, was to do anything that either riled them or helped them. Talk about a tough assignment.

So consider the horror and hatred that raced through Jonah's body as the Lord began revealing and clarifying this ministry command to the prophet's ears. He probably felt equal parts fear and anger.

Nineveh? Never.

Can you imagine how he must have felt? Of course you can. Have you ever been asked to do the one thing you always said you'd "never" do.

- "I'll agree to help, but don't make me speak in public."
- "I'll serve in any capacity, as long as it's not with the homeless."
- "I'll be fine as long as my husband's just one of the church staff, but I never want to be the senior pastor's wife."
- "I'll follow you, Lord, as long as I won't still be single at thirty-five."

We've all got a Nineveh of our own.

For you, it may really be an actual *place* He's calling you to go—a ministry to inner-city youth, to the jail population, to atheists on the Internet, to a certain foreign country. It may be a call to establish relationship with people who think much differently than you do, who share little of your background, who don't run in your typical church circles.

He may be sending you to a particular *person*. He may be calling you to extend forgiveness to someone who has wounded you in profound, life-altering ways—the ex-spouse, the betraying friend, the abusive parent. And the thought of doing so sends you into an emotional tailspin. It feels like such a hopeless assignment, a pointless undertaking. You see nothing good that can come of this. Or maybe you do, but you don't want the responsibility of doing what's required to get there. As far as you're concerned, the only thing that's likely to happen is for you to get hurt, betrayed, and disappointed all over again. You really don't want to go, and like Jonah, you could come up with a million reasons for hanging back or running away.

This is an unwanted interruption. Plain and simple.

And yet "the word of the Lord" has come to you, just as it did with Jonah. God has been continually opening your eyes to Scriptures that point you in this direction. It keeps popping up in Sunday sermons and Bible study groups. Perhaps you came across a program on Christian radio or maybe even a "chance" story you heard on the news or in a movie, and it was like the Spirit prodding your heart, reminding you again what He's been asking you to do.

My friend, this is not an interruption. It's a divine intervention. It's the privilege of walking in fellowship with One who will take you to a hopeless place so you can see the hope of God in its rawest, most redemptive form. He'll take you to an ungodly place so you can see the Holy Spirit rising up within you, transforming an impossible situation while transforming lives in the process. We don't want to go to "Nineveh." Nobody does. But by running and hiding, we miss being part of what God is doing in our day and age.

Like Jonah almost did.

—— The Power of Privilege ——

What's interesting about Jonah's situation is that "the word of the LORD" coming to him (Jon. 1:1) was not the kind we usually see in the lives of other Old Testament prophets. When it appears in most prophetic books, when God is communicating with others of His messengers, "the word" almost always means "the testament" of the Lord. More like a proclamation to be delivered. But in Jonah's case it meant something else—"the instruction" of the Lord.[2] This wasn't just a piece of holy information he was supposed to pass along to others in the course of his usual preaching. This "word" represented a personal mandate that the prophet was supposed to obey himself. And this is what did Jonah in.

It is so much easier to be obedient to God in an advisory capacity only. We're fairly open to telling people how they should handle situations that don't involve our having to pay the price or face the music ourselves. It's a whole lot easier for me to stand up on a platform and tell people what the Bible says and how they're supposed to live than to make sure I'm holding myself to that same standard of living in my everyday life. It's much easier to be consistent about hounding my boys to make their beds every day than it is to pull up the covers on my own.

We look at Jonah and see a man who acted weakly and without conviction. What a coward! What a quitter! But when a similar "instruction" comes our way—when "Nineveh" stands for something that's hard and painful and risky to us personally—we're not usually so quick to hop on board either.

If Jonah had only realized he was experiencing a *divine intervention*, he might have reacted in a more trusting, submissive manner. And if we knew that interruptions often contain the privilege of partnering with God in purposes we could never conceive from our limited vantage point, we might view ours in a different light as well. We might follow Him, trusting Him, even when everything inside is telling us to take the first ship out to sea. Believing that life interruptions—divine interruptions—are a privilege not only causes us to handle them differently but to await them eagerly. Knowing we have an opportunity to participate in God's purposes should cause us to sit on the edge of our seats in anticipation of His next move.

That's how Margaret Stunt has done it. She's a dear woman I ran into while ministering in Australia, and her smile was as bright as the brilliant sun that illuminated Sydney's harbor—which is why I was so shocked to hear of the extremely challenging events she'd recently been facing. It all started while living happily in London, enjoying their daughter's family and four grandchildren nearby, when she and her husband were asked to come be part of a church team in South Africa. Margaret was still rehabbing from knee replacement surgery, so making an international move was naturally out of the question . . . until they were struck by the Spirit's injunction from Hebrews 10:39 not to be like those who "shrink back," but rather like those "who have faith" to follow God wherever He leads, no matter the cost. Despite the many advantages of staying where they were, despite the real and potential hardships of following His call, they remained willing to respond. Free to obey.

It wasn't easy. In addition to the physical strain of travel, they also had to initiate a major downsizing. Yet they did it. They seized upon the interruption as a divine intervention. Giving away most of their belongings except for some clothes, shoes, and photos (and her new dining room chairs!), they left behind home, friends, and family to join God's work in a whole new culture and context.

Their experience in South Africa was hardly without trial and discomfort. Upon their arrival, for example, they found a country experiencing widespread power shortages. Even in their bed-and-breakfast accommodations, the any-minute unknown of available electricity produced creative challenges that made daily life a chore at times—enough to make "shrinking back" an attractive, reflex reaction. Yet God worked richly through them as they continued to embrace the interruption. Among other things, Margaret established a women's ministry at a prison in Pretoria, seeing hundreds of lives changed by the graceful touch of God.

But little more than a year after they'd settled in, the director of Mercy Ministries, a network of homes for troubled young women in several US cities and a few international sites, asked Margaret to consider taking on the executive director role for a proposed new facility in Australia. Sensing God's call to accept, having been close to the outstanding work of Nancy Alcorn and her team in years past, they applied for (and received) four-year visas and packed up for another cross-continental relocation in the late spring.

By the fall, however—soon after Margaret's sixtieth birthday—it became apparent that the Australia home wasn't going to come together. Now was her real chance to stare up into the southern sky and demand an explanation for why these results had happened, to ask how she was supposed to deem this turn of events more desirable than the happy life she'd been living in England before He dragged her several oceans away, leaving her at what appeared to be a failed, depressing conclusion. Instead she clung to the Word, trusting God's promise that He would never extend a command "too difficult" for them to follow (Deut. 30:11) or less profitable than the activities in which they'd been engaged before.

And that's when I ran into her "down under," smiling ear to ear with no reason to be. Despite all that had transpired, despite all the interruptions she'd been dealing with, she was overwhelmingly pleased because now the Lord had led her to a staff position with Hillsong International Leadership College in Sydney—a ministry of the same Hillsong Church known worldwide for its outstanding worship music and heart for God—where she continues to radiate His love and invest her life in reaching the lost and equipping the saints. Sure, it had been a bumpy ride, and the divine interventions had been many, but she's not sure she'd have been in position for this amazing opportunity otherwise.

When we follow God through our interruptions, when we back away from the immediate shock to realize there's more to this issue than meets the eye, we become people who can say (as Margaret does), "We're not sure what our next assignment will be, but we only want to be where God wants us to be."

Is that your true heart's desire?

Then you'll start to see every interruption as a divine intervention.

God's calling of you and me—just like His calling of Margaret Stunt, and of Jonah—means that He has chosen us above anyone else to do what He is asking. It may seem impossible, but you are the one He has singled out and pinpointed as His partner for this particular project. It may seem unbearable to endure, but you are the one through whom He desires to display His glory, even in your own weakness and brokenness. He has purposefully given you the high honor of being one He deems suited for a task with heavenly implications—a divine partnership that will yield magnificent results for you and His kingdom, even if they may not be the splashy and showy variety. That's not the deal. But yielding to His call is. We always succeed when we surrender.

So here was Jonah's instruction: "arise" and "go"—not just to any old place but to Nineveh. A place that seemed to him beyond any hope of restoration. There was nothing Jonah could do there to make any kind of difference, he felt. Yet that's the place God was sending him.

Do you feel like God is asking too much of you? As you scan the landscape of your present circumstances, is it hard to believe this is really what life has brought you to? Does God really expect something promising to come of what you're dealing with, what you're shackled with, what you're stuck with? Could anything be more unwanted or undesirable to you right now?

If He didn't have so much meaning and potential and restoration to accomplish in the midst of it, you're right—it would be a tragic mess. But with everything He wants to achieve through you in this vital yet difficult season, there's another way to look at it.

Consider it a privilege.

CHAPTER 3

Story of Your Life

He restored the border of Israel from the entrance of Hamath as far as the Sea of the Arabah, according to the word of the LORD, the God of Israel, which He spoke through His servant Jonah the son of Amittai, the prophet, who was of Gath-hepher.

2 KINGS 14:25

OK, now, tell me a little about yourself.

You're a certain age. You come from a certain place. You have a certain kind of family—husband, kids, grandkids—or not. You work at a certain job. You live in a certain area or neighborhood. You go to a certain church. That's how we all typically describe ourselves. Details on a résumé. Fill in the blanks.

And that's pretty much how we'll always do it . . . unless something comes along to change our story.

Jonah's biography was no different. From the fine print of 2 Kings 14:25, the only things we learn about him are his given name, his religious background, who his father was, the town he came from, and what he did for a living. Five things. Five nice, ordinary things. And that's it . . . until something came along to radically change his story.

Perhaps *your* life was once neatly defined into catch-all, generic categories. Married. Three children. PTA mom. Taxi cab. Then you became pregnant with your fourth child. And though everything seemed routine and straightforward, suddenly your unborn baby's heart stopped beating at six months. This was no longer the same story you'd been writing before.

Perhaps, like my friend Stephany, your husband was two years into his residency training when he became convinced that God was calling him away from a medical career and into full-time missions. You were all geared up for being married to a doctor. Nice, big house. Private school. Social calendar. You'd already pre-ordered a lifetime supply of nouns and adjectives to describe yourself. And none of them went together to spell "m-i-s-s-i-o-n-a-r-y."

Perhaps your financial plans had always included both of you working until retirement age so your future could line up the way you wanted. Travel. Volunteering. Puttering in the garden. But when you saw your widowed daughter struggling with child-care options for her two young sons, you sensed God was telling you to make yourself available to help. So you quit your job to stay home and watch your grandchildren, even though you weren't sure how you'd handle it, either physically or financially, or what it might mean for later.

Perhaps you were once sensitive about being the last of your siblings to be unmarried, even the two younger than you. But as time has gone on and you've seen so many marriages fail around you—your big brother's, your best childhood friend's, even your own parents' after thirty-eight years—you've grown increasingly wary of what you used to desire so desperately. Just being a fun aunt or uncle is not so bad. So why would God put this woman or this man in your life now, at this age, when you don't even know if marriage is what you want anymore?

In one way or another, your story has developed an unexpected plot twist or two. Or ten. Whether from a spiritual calling of God or a serious complication of life, your plans have been interrupted, and things haven't been the same since. You've been changed forever by this "divine intervention."

In no way do I mean to minimize or downplay the gravity of your personal situation by saying what I'm about to say. But isn't this the dynamic that makes a story so interesting—the change that occurs within characters when they're faced with a hurdle or obstacle in life? Even as far back as freshman English class, they told us that every story hinges around a conflict. Every good movie script, every work of fiction, contains by its nature a crisis—something to be met, wrestled with, and overcome; something that changes a person, a family, a town, even an entire nation. If there's no interruption to the normal, it's just a TV show that airs at 8:00 on Mondays. Just another bland novel with a stock number and a sales price. It takes an interruption, a turning point, to make a story really resonate, to make it something we want to read and watch and tell our friends about.

Think of it. Almost every person in the Bible whose story made a lasting mark faced a sizable interruption in his or her life. They each stood at a crossroad, forced to decide if they would yield to divine intervention or continue ahead on their own path. Beforehand they were just a name on a page. But after it happened, that's when they truly became historic and inspiring.

- *Noah* was interrupted. Snatched out of comfortable obscurity to an uneasy season of challenges with an unknown outcome, he was called by God to build an enormous floating structure he'd never seen or even heard of before. A man who would've otherwise fallen dead and lost among the annals of history became a name still equated with unquestioning faith and rugged obedience.

• *Abraham* was interrupted. Commanded by God to leave his family and friends behind, he embarked on an adventurous journey with few GPS directions but one that ultimately led to the establishment of God's covenant with His chosen people.

• *Sarah* was interrupted. If I thought I was surprised to learn that our third child was on the way, I can only imagine Sarah's shock in hearing that she would give birth to her first son at the ripe old age of ninety. Today, this woman who laughed out loud in disbelief at God's interruption leaves behind her legacy as one of the "holy women" of old "who hoped in God" (1 Pet. 3:5).

• *Joseph* was interrupted. A simple day spent hanging out with his brothers ended up with his being tossed into a pit, left for dead, then sold to traveling slave traders bound for Egypt. Only God could write a story that would take him to the heights of leadership there, rising into position to rescue his forlorn family from a wasting famine.

• *Moses* was interrupted. He was just minding his own business, tending sheep in the Sinai desert, when he was shocked to see the smoke signal of God's presence show up, calling him from tending one flock to leading another (human) one. A wasted, tragic life turned into God's instrument for delivering His people from more than four hundred years of bondage.

• *Christ's disciples* were each interrupted. They were commissioned away from their normal duties, demands, occupations, and relationships in order to throw themselves headlong into following Christ as His closest companions. It would mean persecution and death for all of them yet also the opportunity to walk in intimate fellowship with the Master, inspiring millions more of us to want what they had, to know Jesus at all costs.

- *Mary*, perhaps most of all, was interrupted. She was just making some simple wedding preparations when an angel stopped by to visit, saying, "I've got different plans for you, plans that will make you a personal part of the one defining event in all of human history."
- And *Jonah* . . . Jonah was interrupted. Called from a comfortable life as a prophet in the nation he loved to a God-forsaken country and people group he detested, little did he know the greatest revival in all of human history would involve his individual obedience.

Your life and your interruptions have been superintended by the same God who intervened in the Davids and Esthers and Pauls and Jonahs of Scripture. Not every interruption was pleasant, of course. Few if any of them, even the good ones, came without extraordinary challenges. And yet that's what put these people into position for God to tell a story through them they could never have told before.

What if your most compelling story could only be written with the ink of your latest interruption? Would you live to tell it? Or would you defy God for forcing this plotline on you?

—— A Mess of a Message ——

J. P. hadn't just grown up in church; he had grown up in deep relationship with Christ, diligently seeking the Lord's calling on his life and then finding it as a young navy lieutenant, on mission for God as well as his country.

Today his mission field is a state penitentiary in south central Florida—not as a devoted local church member giving his time to prison ministry but as an inmate on the inside, serving a life sentence with no prospect for parole.

It had been a volatile set of circumstances. He'd recently married a woman who already had two young daughters from a previous marriage. And just when J. P. thought they were settling into life as a loving, blended family, his wife's ex-husband—an alleged abuser—began petitioning the courts for increased custody of their children. All accounts indicated he would ultimately receive a favorable reply, that this man who was deemed by his former wife to be a danger to her girls would now be allowed to take them away from her home at planned intervals. Unsupervised.

What happened in J. P.'s mind as this reality began to draw closer, no one really knows, perhaps not even himself. But one afternoon in broad daylight near an Orlando restaurant, as the Sunday lunch crowd dined inside, J. P. shot and killed this man in the parking lot. By the time the case reached a trial jury, he was declared guilty of first-degree murder. Put away for life.

J. P.'s mom and dad, Gene and Carol Kent, were established, spiritual stalwarts in their church and extended families. Carol's résumé as a Christian writer and highly sought-after speaker meant her bio was a frequent entry on conference schedules and in women's retreat booklets. But Google her name today, and you find much more than book titles, endorsements, and speaking itineraries. You find a story of shock, loss, anguish, disbelief; yet most important, you see the proven, sustaining ironwork of God's power and promises. Even in her new set of circumstances, *A New Kind of Normal*, as one of her recent books titles it—even with her tears often near the surface, she has found a voice she never possessed before.

Prior to this numbing "intervention," a woman might come up to her with a broken heart, appealing to her as the writer, the public speaker, the all-together Christian woman. Carol would probably share her five favorite Scriptures on the comfort of the Holy Spirit, pat her new friend encouragingly on the back, and send her along her way. But these days she might go into the visitors' restroom at the prison after watching her son return to his cell block and find another mother inside, an open faucet of tears raining down her face. She doesn't quote Scripture, doesn't pretend to have every answer. She quietly takes the woman by the hand and hugs her, freely invited into this fellowship of suffering.

Carol's reputation has not preceded her here. She is just another grieving, hurting soul—one of many in this dungeon of clanging doors and lonely echoes. Yet looking into each other's eyes, sharing each other's stories, she discovers something as profound as it is painful: "My mess has become my greatest message."

When she ministers to people today, her story is about the redemption of God, painted against a stark, contrasting canvas of despair, agony, and hopelessness. How easy it would be for Carol to consider her circumstances too shameful to discuss. How much safer to closet herself away from the aching memories and feelings, to put down her pen of testimony, wishing the script could be composed some other way . . . or perhaps never be written at all. But when she stands before groups and individuals these days with her raw self exposed—the anger, the horror, the disappointment, the fear—God tells a story through her that doesn't have to work hard to find an audience. She is no longer just a file in the speakers' bureau, another motivational talk over plates of lemon chicken and snow peas. Her mess creates a message that puts hope back on the table for one person after another, many of whom she'd never otherwise have had an opportunity to reach, for the glory and praise of God.

Every single one of us wants to matter, to make a mark in life that will be remembered long after we're gone—but only on our own terms. We want autonomy, independence, and the freedom to govern our own steps. We don't mind Christ getting involved, as long as His path eventually converges onto the one we'd already chosen anyway. We want to select our own course, chase our own ambitions, and decide what stands out when people think of us.

But then the unwanted and unexpected happens. God calls you to Nineveh. A minister who once anticipated preaching to thousands each Sunday now toils at a church where forty-five is a really big crowd. A mother who trained to be the chairman of IBM is now the CEO of H-O-M-E. This is not the job history profile she imagined for herself.

So what do we do? How do we handle the deviations of life that don't match the script we'd prepared for ourselves? Maybe, just maybe, if we'll go along with God on this, we'll see Him setting us up to make our mark.

—— That'll Leave a Mark ——

I'm a preacher's kid—not just some preacher from some church on some corner somewhere, but a preacher and church that is literally known around the globe. And when I was a wee one, I had a knack for making sure other people knew it. My lifelong childhood friends tell me that whenever I wanted to assert some type of authority or control, I was quick to remind them who my dad was. (How obnoxious of me. I'm surprised I still have any friends at all after those annoying young years.)

And while I'd like to think I've been humbled these decades later, I know what it means to form one's identity and significance from facts on a bio sketch. I've always known that a big part of who I am comes from my deep legacy of family and faith, and I'm sincerely grateful for it. But the temptation for me now could easily be to consider myself covered, to think I can always ride in air-conditioned comfort underneath the built-in structure of reputation and connections.

And yet the story God is writing with my life—the mark He wants me to make on this generation and the next—cannot be based solely on information found on my birth certificate or my lifelong membership status in the church where my father serves. The people I love are doing the work God has assigned to them—and doing it with great humility and faithfulness, producing harvest after harvest of spiritual fruit. But my mark must be mine. *Built* on the past but also uniquely my own in the present and future.

Perhaps you can relate to that. You've been trying to stake your claim to significance on a list of accomplishments and attributes boasted on your résumé, a docket of background facts and figures—who you are, where you're from, what you do for a living, the success you've been having, the family you've been raising. These are all good things. Blessings worth celebrating. But if you force these line items of life to bear the weight of your personal value, you'll be rudely disappointed at many points along the way. They are not built to carry that load. Stray bullet points do not ascribe worth and significance to us all by themselves.

Perhaps, on the other hand, your issue is not with an overinflated sense of entitlement but rather a history of shame and sensitivity to what your background information contains. Maybe, like me in certain seasons of life, you're *not* proud of the people you've associated with or the places you've been. Maybe you've *not* achieved as much as you'd like or at the level of those around you. From where you sit today, you don't see how your life could tell any other story than that of failure, lost opportunities, and the bitter results of not getting the breaks.

Or maybe you just feel ordinary. With a Jonah-like résumé. Uneventful. Kind of like the way I enjoy my yogurt . . . plain vanilla without any of the crunchy, colorful toppings. No huge successes. No huge flame-outs. Just one average day after another, with not much to tell on the other side.

But none of this really matters in the long run. Thank God, it neither *exempts* you nor *disqualifies* you from finding real significance the only way it can be found—by yielding, submitting, and fully surrendering to God's purposes. It's the same for everybody. Complete satisfaction and success in life cannot be reached apart from your deliberate decision to engage in the divine intervention and surrender to His sovereign plans for you, whatever He chooses those plans to be.

Because, see, we're not here to tell *our* story. We're here to tell God's story. And none of us are too good, too cultured, too Christianized, or too impressive for Him to thread any plotline He desires through our lives, even if that plotline has a destination like Nineveh in it. God maintains just as much right to throw curves into my life as He does into anybody else's, no matter who my parents are or what church I go to. By the same token, none of us are too weak, too disadvantaged, too invisible, or too unimportant for Him to speak something of great, eternal value through our experiences. Neither our legacy nor the lack thereof determines our self-worth and significance. It is God's calling and our willingness to obey. That's it.

We could draw it up on the board like this:

Divine Intervention + Yielded Submission =
Eternal Significance

Significance. Each of us is searching for it. The woman I met who was devastated after being passed over for a promotion (again)—she's looking for it. Monica, the waitress at Planet Hollywood bemoaning her broken heart over her barely there boyfriend, is looking for it. The homemaker I was talking to recently is looking for it—the feeling of significance that's often swept away underneath the pile of details and demands from her full life. Deep down we're *all* looking for it. We all want to matter. As believers in the Lord Jesus, we each want to know that God has called us to make some kind of difference, something that gives us a level of value and significance in the big picture.

And wouldn't you know it, the interrupted life is the cure for that search.

I'm serious. When God speaks, when He intervenes, when He permits a circumstance to rise up around you, it is your opportunity to write a story that people may still be talking about many years from now. Like those holy heroes of old from Scripture, your story of divine intervention—the one that brought you to your knees in frustration—could be the very thing that lifts others' eyebrows in wonder and amazement at your strength and tenacity, the one that causes them to see the sparkle of substance, significance, and impact in your life. This could be the part of your story that encourages another to make their own decision to follow hard after God, perhaps rewriting the lines for their whole family, replacing a legacy of rebellion with a future of trusting faithfulness.

So just go with it. Follow Him—impossible as it may seem. Let Him take you places, even to places you honestly don't feel all that great about seeing firsthand. You may not grasp what He's got in mind for this, but if you'll follow where He's leading, you will walk yourself right out onto the stage He has set for you. You will locate a significance bigger than you are because it's not based on your own smarts and planning and goal strategies but rather on your utter submission to the Father's eternal, all-wise plans—plans that are "higher than your ways" (Isa. 55:9), beyond anything you could "ask or think" or imagine (Eph. 3:20).

Oh, I know it can be extremely challenging sometimes. Gut-wrenching and intense. Perhaps you've never faced anything this daunting before, a situation that asks so much of you or hurts in such deep places. But with the Red Sea in front of you and Pharaoh's armies barrelling down close behind, you get to find out what the Lord can really do. He's put you in a tough spot so you'll get to see just how incredibly strong and sufficient your God is.

And others will see it too.

Your life is God's story being told and His character being displayed. So how does it read? What does it tell others about the God you serve? Will you dare to believe there's a message in this mess? It's quite possibly the best story some people will ever read.

— Writer's Night —

Truly there was more to Jonah than he realized. He wasn't merely "Jonah the son of Amittai, the prophet, who was of Gath-hepher" (2 Kings 14:25). He was a child of God in the center of a divine intervention. And a whole people group was about to feel the power of what that meant.

Yes, the command God had given him was *different* than the one He'd given to some of Jonah's contemporaries—men like Amos and Hosea. Their job was to stay within the comfy confines of their beloved nation of Israel and minister to their own people. Jonah's new job, on the other hand, was to leave home and safety and to speak God's message to a savage population hundreds of miles away.

In addition, Jonah could also make the case that his calling was more *difficult* than what others were being assigned. Other prophets had their challenges, to be sure, but they weren't being told to walk into a butchery in a pagan nation where the audience was already predisposed to detest you. If the Ninevites didn't look kindly on Jonah's message—and it sure didn't seem like they would—he'd soon have a cold body to match their cold shoulder. You don't go out railing against the wickedness of your enemies in their own public square with no back up behind you in case the worst happens.

Have you looked at other people around you and wondered why you've been asked to endure a route that appears different and more difficult than theirs? Are you wondering why everybody else gets such an easy time of it while you're left to struggle with something so hard to handle? Are you asking, "Why would God do this to me?"

But, see, your significance is at stake. He's reworking our bland résumés as we speak. He has asked us to walk this road because it's the one through which a homemaker, a single woman, a math major, a grandmother, a country girl, a tax preparer, a first cousin, or a part-time employee becomes a person with a story more remarkable than her résumé, a story only God can tell.

You are not just an information form. Not just data entries and check boxes. You are the precious child of a living, heavenly Father who intervenes that you might show forth His greatness and glory. Your life may be a bit distressing at the moment or more overwhelming than you'd prefer, but this is the setting where God's creativity turns ordinary people into timeless classics.

Therefore, you are neither confined by your résumé nor allowed to hide yourself behind it. Like Jonah, there's more to you than you realize. And this interruption—I mean, intervention—may be where you find that out.

Hold high the inkwell. He's on to something. Let Him write.

Part 2

On the Run

CHAPTER 4

Beyond a Reasonable Doubt

But Jonah rose up to flee to Tarshish from the presence of the LORD.

JONAH 1:3

According to estimates from the sporting goods industry, as many as thirty to forty million Americans are at least occasional runners, with something like ten million who say they run frequently and consistently. The famous Boston Marathon hosts a field of up to twenty-five thousand every spring, and it seems like more people than ever are finding some kind of long-distance race to enter these days, somehow managing to force themselves past the finish line—26.2 miles away. I don't know how they do it.

I mean, I like to run . . . a little. But I'm hardly what you'd call a "runner." Sounds so prestigious, doesn't it—being a real live, serious "runner"? And yet I own up to falling short of that glorious and auspicious title because my interest lies more in the hours after having *finished* a short run than in the actual run itself—when my side's quit hurting, when I've had a shower, and I feel like I've earned myself a few extra calories! My reason for run-ning is clear, simple, and fairly straightforward: I want to eat and still be able to slide into my Gap jeans. OK? So there. Superficial, I know, but you can't accuse me of not being honest with you.

Nobody runs without a reason. Maybe it's to lose weight. Or to build endurance and stamina. Or to get back into their swim-suit. For some people, running just makes them feel good. (I'm not sure I really believe that, but . . .) They like the way the breeze feels on their face. They like pushing themselves. They like build-ing up to their second wind, experiencing that moment when they break through the struggle and feel as if they could do this all day long.

Every runner has a reason.

And Jonah certainly had his.

When God's call came along for him to "go to Nineveh the great city and cry against it, for their wickedness has come up before Me," the reasons colliding in Jonah's mind seemed to leave him with no other choice: he "rose up to flee to Tarshish from the presence of the LORD" (Jon. 1:2–3).

His first reason for running was a matter of *allegiance*. Jonah was what you'd call a hypernationalist, an elitist, a patriot in regard to the Israelite people. And the very idea that God would be showing any interest at all in a Gentile nation went counter to every true-north setting on Jonah's spiritual compass.

This was not merely a political stand on his part; it was how he honestly interpreted God's word and message through the centuries of their cultural history. People like the Ninevites sim-ply did not belong within the flowing stream of God's mercy. Israel was the sole owner of His blessing and favor, and therefore this notion that God's attention might be turned toward outsid-ers was absolute absurdity. A breach of loyalty. To answer this call of God, Jonah would hardly be able to live within his own skin, much less deal with what his like-minded fellow citizens would think of him.

Knowing God as he did—being a prophet as he was—he had a good idea (according to Jonah 4:2) that this little one-man preaching crusade God was proposing could easily result in a noticeable change of heart by these heartless killers who had become Israel's sworn enemies. And if that was God's intention in sending him—if He insisted on making Jonah choose between obeying the Lord and being true to his native people—Jonah was choosing his people every time. That's where his true allegiance was.

Sometimes the divine intervention of God means breaking allegiance with what you love. Maybe it's some goal you've been hanging onto for years: a house with a few acres of land in the country, a certain level of income—your ticket to building out that space over the garage to make a big den and entertainment room, or the picture of "family" you've been forming in your mind.

Maybe it's a professional ambition—a wish to become self-employed, to finally write that book you've always thought was inside you, to move to New York or Los Angeles and take a real chance at fulfilling your dream. But these aren't proving to be the tasks or directions God wants you to undertake. He knows of better things, more fruitful things, places where His blessing is sure to follow if you go there.

You always thought you knew where you were headed. But now your life's been interrupted, and these personal goals, hopes, and trajectories are being asked to take a backseat to what God uniquely has in mind for you.

So what's it gonna be? *Your* plans? *Your* loves? Or His? Where does your allegiance lie?

A good way to determine this is to see how you respond to a divine intervention, especially one that costs you something you don't want to part with (which many of them do). Will you go with God even when He's calling you to "Nineveh," even if Nineveh goes against everything you want to be doing right now? That's a question you'll either yield to or run from. It's not going to be easy, whichever way you choose. But one choice holds the promise of being strangely contented in God's will; the other, well—it can get a little fishy.

In addition to his allegiance issues, Jonah's second set of reasons for running had more to do with *logic*. God's instructions just didn't make sense to him . . . for a *couple* of reasons. First, if the scholars have their map skills right, the trip to Nineveh would've been a tough one to make. Nineveh was approximately five hundred miles to the east of where Jonah was currently located in Jerusalem,[3] meaning it might have been a journey he never returned from in his lifetime—even if he wasn't murdered on sight the minute he got there and opened his mouth. He most likely would've needed to sell all his earthly possessions to make the trip, leaving behind the economic security and familiarity of his beloved country to venture into this pagan land. Why would God have allowed him to accumulate all of this, only to get rid of it?

Simply made no sense.

Second, Jonah's whole ministry (as we've seen) had been focused on foretelling Israel's expansion and prosperity. Up until now, this had been his divine mission. This is what enthused him. This is what he was most zealous for. This is what made him willing to pace the floor at night, listening for the voice of God to show him how all of this was going to come about. He didn't want to play any role in the possibility that the Ninevites might respond to news of God's judgment and receive His mercy because that would've stood in the way of Israel's returning to a state of growth and stability. So Jonah probably felt quite justified in his anti-Nineveh position. Going there seemed contrary to what he thought God desired for His people. Going to Nineveh and contributing to their health and thriving success were not on his prayer list.

Simply made no sense.

We've probably all received a nudge from God before to undertake a task or challenge that didn't square with what seemed logical to us. For example, we know His Word talks about us being generous, giving people. But surely He's aware that we're trying to put a little money aside for our kids' education, that one of our cars is barely running, that the tax bill is coming due whether the church raises enough money for their new building fund or not.

You may have heard Him telling you—as I've been encouraging Bible study groups to do—to accept His call to reach out to a modern-day "Nineveh," some project or person that seems out of reach from the gospel or seems in some way undeserving of love and divine mercy because of their grotesque past and horrendous choices. And yet, frankly, attending this one hour of Bible study each week is about all the time you can spare from the responsibilities you've got already with home and work and family and everything. If people knew what your Saturdays were like with ball games and laundry and grocery shopping, they'd be glad you had enough energy to make it to church on Sunday at all, much less to crowd another obligation on top of your crazy schedule.

Or maybe instead of a direct, spiritual appeal from God, the thing that makes the least sense in your life right now is some circumstance—some interruption—that's cropped up at the worst possible time. I mean, you didn't need your husband to get hurt on the assembly line and miss six months of work, at only a partial wage, not with a daughter needing braces and now having to pay a neighbor boy to take care of the yard all summer.

Doesn't make any sense.

Oh, yes, Jonah had his reasons for running. He couldn't make sense of what he was hearing. Couldn't compute this odd directive with what his heart had always told him in the past, with what his prior allegiances dictated. Couldn't go along with God's command and keep his personal hopes and dreams alive.

Maybe, though, Nineveh wasn't really what Jonah was running from.

—— The Great Escape ——

Yes, Jonah had his reasons. His allegiances were in question. His logic was being challenged. But to understand the true core of what motivated Jonah to take to the high seas in fleeing God's command, I only need to think back to my teenage years. See, I wasn't the easiest child for my parents to raise. If they ever sat up worrying at night, it was usually because of something I had said or done. I was not exactly a stranger to rebellion, and I worked really hard to keep most of the ugly details from my mom and dad.

I remember being at home one ordinary day during that time—one of those offhand scenes from the past that has no reason for being etched so deeply into my memory except for the fact that . . . it is. Nothing special was going on. Wasn't a deliberately eventful moment. I was just sitting in the den next to my daddy, watching television.

I really don't think he knew at the time exactly what I had been doing. It wasn't something we had previously discussed, hadn't been a matter for discipline. But sitting there with the TV on, just the two of us, with nobody saying a word, this intense surge of conviction strangely began pulsing through me. My stomach started knotting up, my hands got sweaty, tears welled in my eyes. Something was happening to me merely from being in the same room with my dad, who loved me so much and would never push me away if I came to him repenting. I touched him on the arm, turned to look into his face, and simply said, "Daddy, I'm so sorry for what I've done."

Just being alone in his presence—the presence of my father—I was undone. It changed me.

I can't help but think that with Jonah being so near to *his* Father's presence, God's unbelievable holiness must have had this same kind of effect. When we're in the presence of Almighty God Himself, the sense of distinction between the two of us, the searchlight He casts on even the slightest hint of rebellion—it can be too much to handle. It can undo you and threaten to trip you up, like an untied shoelace flopping around a toddler's shoe. If you're not prepared or looking for it, this intense holiness can make you want to run away.

Not just from His Word but from *Him*.

Pour all of Jonah's reasons and rationales in a mixing bowl, stir them together so everyone can see how thick and substantial they are, and then let's just cut through the cookie dough, shall we? Jonah wasn't really running from what God was saying, implying, suggesting, demanding.

He was running from God.

Running from His authority, His accountability, His holiness.

And Jonah, of all people, should have known better than this—this "running from the Lord" business. After all, this wasn't his first time around the religious block. He was well acquainted with the workings of the Lord. He knew God couldn't be escaped. He was part of a rare breed of elite men called to be prophets, of which there were perhaps fewer than fifty in Israel during all the years between the time of Moses and Malachi. These men were "chosen for their sensitivity to God. Jonah must have been an impressive man, steeped in wisdom and insight, walking closely with the Lord."[4] He knew the truth about God. He knew that running from Him was a futile effort. He knew God to be omnipresent—everywhere at the same time, no less in one location than He is in another, always where Jonah was at any moment of any given day. So why would he even bother to consider this running thing?

Yet that's just what he did. "Jonah rose up to flee to Tarshish from the presence of the LORD" (Jon. 1:3). This phrase in the original language, "from the presence of," comes from the Hebrew word *milliphne*. It refers to a person coming out of an official audience with the king. In Genesis 41:46, the same word is used in speaking of Joseph as he went out "from the presence of" Pharoah into the land of Egypt.[5] The implication of *milliphne* is that Jonah was not merely running from the "word of the Lord" but was trying to steer clear of having a one-on-one, face-to-face encounter with Him. He wanted to put distance between himself and Jerusalem, the place where God's tangible presence rested with His people. He didn't want to hear His voice or be aware of His nearness.

Jerusalem—the epicenter of Jewish life, the city where the temple of God stood, the place where God's presence hung out. Yes, God was certainly omnipresent enough to be in Joppa, Jericho, Tarshish, or Timbuktu, all at the same time. But Jerusalem was the seat of God's *manifest presence*, the place where the altar was, where the ark of the covenant was, where atonement for sin took place, where the prophets and priests heard His voice and felt most attuned to what He was doing in their midst. God was everywhere, of course, but in Jerusalem God made His presence known.

And that made Jerusalem a little too close for Jonah's comfort.

Call it what you like, we sometimes just don't want to look Him in the eye. Our running is really a vain attempt to keep from having to deal with a holy God and His sovereign authority.

The other day I asked my oldest son, Jackson, to help me straighten up the bathroom. But he didn't want to help me straighten up the bathroom. *Didn't make any sense to him* that a bathroom would need to be any cleaner than it already was. Didn't want to be interrupted, you see. And while he knew he couldn't stop this towering woman with the sponges and spray bottles from roaming through the house, he did think he could at least escape having an official audience with her. Next thing I know, he's not in front of the television watching cartoons any more, out in broad daylight. Instead he's tucked up in the closet next to his toy box, having risen up to flee "from the presence of"—*milliphne*—the cleaning lady.

That's what Jonah was hoping to do.

And did he ever go to some great lengths to do it.

So he earned it. That prestigious title of "runner." Man, did he earn it.

—— Tarshish ——

No one knows for sure where Tarshish was—this place Jonah decided to make a break for. But the best guess is that it was a Phoenician colony off the coast of Spain. And clearly it was in the opposite direction of Nineveh. By a long shot. If Nineveh was five hundred miles to the east of Joppa, then Tarshish was approximately *two thousand* miles west, "as far in that direction toward the end of the world as a man could go in that day."[6] To a person living in ancient Israel, it might have been considered the farthest point you could travel without dropping off the map.

But why Tarshish? This certainly wasn't the only option available to Jonah. If he'd already decided to disobey, he sure could've done it with a lot less cost and inconvenience.

He could've just stayed put, for example. Certainly would've been a lot simpler. Even if this meant taking a hit to his proper prophet status or going into a sort of self-imposed retirement, he still could sleep in his own bed at night.

Or if he didn't want to stay in Israel, he at least could've chosen a getaway port that was a lot more commutable from home. There were closer, neighboring towns that were easier to get to and less dramatic to navigate. He didn't have to sail clear off to the edge of the known world. While either of these scenarios would have been equally disobedient as running for Tarshish— (let's be clear about *that*)—they would've been a whole lot easier to make happen.

Plus, some commentators believe when he "went down to Joppa, found a ship which was going to Tarshish, paid the fare and went down into it" (Jon. 1:3), he didn't just buy his own passage but actually rented out the entire boat so he could guarantee complete control over when and how fast the boat got there.[7] So going to Tarshish was an extreme choice that would've been quite a pricey affair, yet one he apparently deemed worth the cost.

Nowhere's far enough, and no price is too steep when you're running from God.

If my two-year-old's verbal skills could keep up, he'd explain this concept to us because he knows a thing or two about running. He seems to have earned some type of secret society degree, perhaps bestowed by the underground School of Running and Escapism that's apparently trained every two-year-old on the planet. He's a true expert in running . . . from *me*. If I move one step in his direction when he's not wanting to be caught, he takes off with a smirk on his face and an uncanny quickness in his step. Yup, Jude could tell you in a heartbeat how Jonah just desperately wanted to put Jerusalem as far in his rearview mirror as possible, the way my son often tries to do with me.

Tarshish, here we come!

One of the ways you and I can test whether or not we're on the run from God is to see if we're trying to get away from the places where His manifest presence hangs outs. Are you staying away from church? Even if you're still attending, do you slip into the back at the last minute, then hit the exits as quickly as you can, hoping to avoid having to deal up-close with anyone? Have you dropped out of your Bible study group, growing a little more uncomfortable with where the conversations were headed and how close they were hitting to home? Have you slacked off your time in the Word and in prayer, always finding something better and more urgent to do—something that doesn't hold you so accountable, doesn't feel so convicting.

God's continuous presence is a soothing balm to the hurting, a sweet relief for the broken and betrayed, a haven for those who find themselves feeling strangely out of tune with the music of this world. But to those living in disobedience, to those who don't want to submit to their current circumstances and see what God might want to accomplish through them, His presence is a scorching fire. We duck our eyes to keep from coming face-to-face with Him. We slip down a side hallway. We go the long way around.

We run.

But sometimes in ways nobody else could notice.

Yes, we know all kinds of running strategies. Often in an attempt to coddle our consciences and maintain our reputations, we make ourselves go through the motions. We write out the tithe check, figuring that God can't argue with hard math even if our heart's not in it. We raise our kids, but we're disgruntled with every task. We serve people, but we're secretly mad at God for making us put up with this whole thing. We pretend in public as though we care about what everybody tells us we're *supposed* to

care about. We put one foot in front of the other, but we're grip-
ing and mouthing about it the whole time—to ourselves if not to
others. We show up at church, on the job, to the monthly "date
night" with our other single friends or for another full day of
mothering, but we're not all there, not fully engaged in the task
and season of life at hand.

We're running on the inside—running away mentally, running
away emotionally, even running away spiritually, painting on a
Sunday smile while privately resisting the fellowship God wants,
mad that He's doing this to us, mad that we've been blocked and
interrupted from the life we really want. If God won't take care of
our deepest concerns, won't shield us from pain or loss or challenge or boredom, we'll just take care of ourselves, doing what we
must to survive—with Him or (if He persists in withholding what
we want) *without* Him.

But in running—even if it's the inside, unseen kind—we place
ourselves in the worst possible position we could be in. We stand
outside of God's will, outside of His blessing. For even the more
discreet, culturally acceptable methods of running are equally disobedient, just like when we say, "I know what the Bible says about
that, but . . ." Oooo, be careful when those words bubble up out
of your heart. They mean the starting gun has fired, and a runner
has taken off.

What God was saying to Jonah—"Go to Nineveh the great
city and cry against it" (v. 2)—didn't make any sense to him. From
how the Bible describes it, he didn't appear to spend even one second mulling it over. The word of the Lord came, Jonah hopped up
in a huff, and headed for the nearest shipyard. Like ourselves too
often, he wasn't willing to consider that something so apparently
illogical could be the precise will of God for him at that moment
in time, that doing anything less would not only result in a costly
detour but in missing out on the miracle God had planned.

We just cannot comprehend, as God can, why He has met us with this piece of conviction right now or placed us in the midst of this circumstance. So the determining factor we use in choosing obedience over disobedience—in choosing surrender over stubborn resistance—can never be our finite ability to understand His directives. Making sense of God's call is not a prerequisite for following it. His Word and His promises are enough.

Have you already packed your bags for Tarshish? Have you been trying as hard as you can to avoid being seen in the places where God's presence is most tangibly felt? Have you closed off any likelihood that this interruption might ultimately lead you to somewhere of divine importance? Are you trying to get as far away as possible from what He's called you to do, disengaging emotionally and energetically if not physically?

Even if this chapter has caught you in midflight, it's not too late to turn your ship around and sail back in the direction of His will. It might not make sense to everybody. It might not even make sense to you. But this I know for sure. In fact, I know it beyond any reasonable doubt. Heading back to the mainland of obedience will be the best decision of your life.

CHAPTER 5

Slippery Slope

So he went down to Joppa, found a ship which was going to Tarshish, paid the fare and went down into it to go with them to Tarshish from the presence of the LORD.

JONAH 1:3

"It wasn't this bad in the beginning."

I sat across the table from her, listening to the chapters of her life story unfold like a bad movie. Each new scene spun another tale from a life that had fully spun out of control. She'd given in to an addiction, countless illicit relationships, and a host of other horrid decisions, leaving her with a crippled life and an aching heart. In a last, desperate attempt to salvage what remained of her wounded potential, she had entered a treatment program and was now living in a transitional home, praying for a fresh start.

As she shared with me her personal saga—so full of sadness and searching and unsavory characters—she almost seemed in disbelief at the path her life had taken, as if this woman she was describing couldn't possibly be the same girl she'd always known herself to be on the inside.

One after another the hurtful revelations spilled from her broken spirit until, finally, she leaned back in her chair, turned her head to one side, stared blankly out the window, and said in almost a whisper—to me, to herself, to no one in particular—"If I'd only known where those first few decisions would lead me, maybe I would've chosen differently."

Those first decisions. Those first choices.

They really are so critical.

I think all of us can relate to that. As a kid, whenever I was caught in a bit of disobedience, I always had a tendency to try lying my way out of trouble. It seemed like a shortcut to safety, an easy way to avoid punishment. Making up a story usually covered me for a while, maybe long enough (I hoped) to get away with it completely. But almost without fail—don't we all know?—one lie leads to another; a second lie must be parlayed into a third. Each one I told always positioned me on a steeper, more slippery part of the slope, closer to the edge, forcing me to be ever more meticulous about what I said next and how it squared with what I'd said before. How much simpler it would've been if I'd have just told the truth from the start. There was really no good way now for this to end.

No way out except . . . down.

But like my young friend said, this is not the way it seems in the beginning. Before things go bad, it's just a night that sounds like a lot of fun. A day that feels like wasting. A risk that looks like something we can likely handle, a limb that'll probably hold our weight. We don't think getting back home will be a problem when we're finished. After all, we're not going far.

Not until we're well down the mountain, much too far to pull ourselves easily back up to the top, we realize we've gotten ourselves into a mess. Instead of three or four good ways to get back on our feet, we now have maybe one—or none—none that don't come without a long, hard process, without a good bit of shame and embarrassment, none we can do on our own without a lot of help from others, none that won't cost us.

We look at ourselves and know it didn't have to be this way. We had our chances. Could've chosen differently. Didn't have to settle. Should've listened to what others were telling us, what we knew in our heart to be right.

But that's what comes of running. It starts with a few steps, picks up speed; and before we know it, we're like a certain prophet of God I know who woke up one stormy day acting like anything *but* one.

—— On the Way Down ——

The second Jonah determined God's call to Nineveh was not up his alley, the moment he decided God's word wasn't something he was necessarily required to obey, he essentially resigned his position as a prophet. No one who legitimately claims to speak for God can fail to listen when God speaks. Jonah was stepping down from his office.

But notice, as you follow this narrative through the next few verses that follow, how many more times this idea of going "down" is used in relation to Jonah's actions.

- *"He went down to Joppa" (v. 3).* Joppa (modern-day Jaffa) was one of the major ports in the ancient Near East. Assuming he went there from Jerusalem, it meant a journey of about thirty miles, descending from the mountainous terrain of Israel's inland regions to the coastal, sea-level elevations on the Mediterranean. It was a downhill run. For him, a downhill sprint.
- *"[He] found a ship which was going to Tarshish, paid the fare and went down into it" (v. 3).* Stepping off dry land, he

continued his flight from God's calling by going "down" into the boat as a runaway passenger.

- *"Jonah had gone below into the hold of the ship" (v. 5).* Once on board, he didn't stand topside to watch the waves go by but headed down to the lower bunks to get some sleep.

Down. Down. Always down. Eventually down to the bottom of the sea, into the belly of the big fish. His decision to run from God's command, to escape God's manifest presence, spun a web of disaster from which he couldn't be freed. Before he knew it, his circumstances had gained an unstoppable momentum, taking on a life of their own. Soon he was in the teeth of a ferocious sea storm, had been fingered by the sailors as the likeliest cause of this fury, then was hurled into the lightning-charged waters. Apparently "down" for the count.

Such is life for those of us who make that first decision to resist what God has in mind for His *divine interventions.*

King David, for example, saw the calendar turn to spring one year a little earlier than he was ready for. During this period in history, spring marked the traditional time "when kings go out to battle" (2 Sam. 11:1). But David evidently saw this as an *interruption* to his previous plans. For whatever reason, he just didn't go that year. He sent his military commander Joab to take care of the war plans in his place.

David was . . . well, *King David.* The giant killer. The psalm writer. The one who twice had acted with God-fearing restraint in not taking the life of his nemesis, King Saul, when he could've. The one whom God had described as "a man after His own heart" (1 Sam. 13:14), who had subdued Israel's longtime enemies and received the covenant promise of God: "Your house and your kingdom shall endure before Me forever" (2 Sam. 7:16). He was the last person on earth, you'd think, who would do something to foul this up or even be capable of such a thing.

But if anyone knows how a few bad decisions can leave behind a huge mess to clean up, it's King David.

You surely know the story. First, as mentioned, he opted out of a responsibility so he could hang back home at the palace. Then, while (perhaps innocently enough) taking a late-night stroll around his rooftop during a bout of wakefulness, he spied a beautiful woman taking a bath in some nearby location down below. Talk about an explosive combination—a moonlit night, an undressed woman, a lonely man of power, influence, and persuasion. All the elements were in place for a fall from grace.

At this point David had an option. He could have marched himself back to bed, tried to clear his head of the temptation, and tell himself to wake up in the morning refocused on the self-discipline and priorities that had led him to greatness. Instead he chose to linger on that rooftop. Chose to breathe the oxygen that allowed his lusts to spark into flame. Unable to stop himself from desiring what he'd set in motion, he sent a messenger to invite the woman up to his room (after discovering that her warrior husband was away in battle) and slept with her.

From there, those first, fateful decisions led to a desperate cover-up, a senseless murder, the ordeal of watching his illegitimate son's death, a lifelong loss of trust and relationship with his children, and—always most importantly—the displeasure of God: "The thing that David had done was evil in the sight of the LORD" (2 Sam. 11:27).

Wonder how stunned David was as he considered the downward spiral of events in his life. Wonder how many times he thought back to that starry night on the rooftop, the same starry sky he could have been scanning from outside his tent on the battlefield, doing his duty.

One bad decision can take a person down.

Jesus painted a similar story in his parable of the prodigal son. This young man who couldn't wait for the opportunity to stake claim to his inheritance—who would not allow this interrupting interval in his life to become a season of patience and character building—found out the hard way how far down the satisfaction ladder you can fall when you take that first, headstrong leap into selfish entitlement. Leaving behind the safety of his home and the love of his father, this prodigal runaway (much like Jonah) set his sights on a "distant country" (Luke 15:13), choosing rebellion over obedience. Before long he was looking up from the squalor of a filthy pigsty, wondering how his visions of carefree happiness had turned so quickly into hog slop.

I know he's not the only one.

During my years at the University of Houston, I developed a relationship with a young man who wasn't a Christian. While I told him flat-out I couldn't get serious with someone who didn't know the Lord, my actions told a much different story. Spend enough time letting your heart become drawn in by someone you're starting to like more and more, and all those noble guide-lines you brought from home and church and family can turn into *dotted* lines—ones that bend and weaken toward what you want. Ones that tend to perforate when push comes to shove.

Before I knew it, I was emotionally attached. Locked into a roller-coaster ride I couldn't seem to get off, no matter how hard I tried. But one thing I should've known about roller coasters: they usually take a hard, downward turn when you're least expect-ing it.

How clearly I remember the night we were out on a date and ended up at one of his friend's houses. Even as our front tires wheeled into the driveway, I knew I was in the wrong place. Cars were lined up everywhere. All the sights and sounds of a raucous, off-campus college party were evident with one glance. Empty beer cans and liquor bottles were scattered on the lawn. Loud music blaring from the windows. The acrid stench of drugs in the air.

He grabbed my hand and led me in.

Surely there's a difference in appearance between a genuinely happy smile and the plastered grin I painted on myself as he introduced me around. When offered a drink of this and a smoke of that, I tried to look casual in declining, but I'm sure I couldn't disguise all the discomfort I was feeling. I had never felt like that with this guy before. But now—here—in this rowdy, darkened, mind-spinning situation, I experienced my prodigal pigsty moment. "How did I end up in a place like this?"

Easy—from that first decision to enter into relationship with a guy who didn't value my belief system, who didn't understand what I was really all about.

First decisions. Acceptable compromises. Lazy judgment calls that don't feel like any big deal at the time. Rejections of Christ's lordship in areas that seem like only minor disobediences.

They're some of the first things Satan latches onto when he believes he's got a hot prospect for taking down. Those initial urges of ours to run from God's Word, to resist His divine plans and opportunities for us, are how lusts and desires of every kind give "birth to sin; and when sin is accomplished, it brings forth death" (James 1:15).

The decisions you're making today will impact your tomorrows. (Mind if I say that again?) The way you respond to the interruptions you're facing right now will have a bearing on the direction your life takes next. A year from now, a decade from now, a generation from now, you'll know whether or not you've walked with God in a faithful, trusting manner or whether you've left yourself wide open to doubt and bitterness and all the biting regrets of picking and choosing your obedience options.

Every David who sneaks up onto the rooftop for another look will end up trapped in a web of deception. Every prodigal son who thinks he knows more about life than his "Father" will find himself in a pigsty. And every Jonah who runs in the opposite direction of God's calling will see the storm clouds gathering behind him. It's only a matter of time.

Down. Down. Always down.

—— Hard to See ——

I'm willing to bet you know what I'm talking about. In fact, it may be fairly likely that you're reading these words today from somewhere far down that slippery slope. And because our enemy loves seeing you there, he tries everything he knows to keep you from realizing where you are, to make this free fall feel somehow enjoyable—like you've gotten away with something and you're none the worse for it. He can make you so unaware of being in the tumble cycle that you think it's a place to rest and relax.

Asleep in the storm.

"How is it that you are sleeping?" the terrified sea captain shouted over the howling winds (Jon. 1:6) when they found him cuddled up napping in the lower deck. I guess I have the same question. How could a man who knew exactly how he got here, knew exactly what he'd done, knew exactly who he was running from and what his God was capable of—how could he possibly be so oblivious to what was going on?

Exhausted? Maybe. I'm sure it had been a long, stressful day with all that running around and trip planning. Sin and guilt have a way of affecting you physically (see Ps. 32:1–5). *Escape?* Sometimes I've used sleep almost like a drug to make the pain and worry go away, hoping things will look better in the morning. *Depressed?* He may have been so resigned to his fate, he'd quit caring what others thought or what was going to happen to him next. *Justified?* Perhaps he was basically so sure about the rightness of his position on this Nineveh thing that he'd become comfortable within himself and was convinced he was taking the high road. He wasn't about to let a little rain and high wind rattle his convictions or keep him up at night.

May have been any or all of these things. A combination of factors. But my mother sense tells me it was probably something else.

As a mom to three young, scrappy boys, I am often overwhelmingly tired at the end of the day. Yet if any one of them makes the slightest peep in the middle of the night, I am on my feet and in their rooms almost before I know that I'm standing and walking upright. Fatigue doesn't always keep me from reacting quickly and alertly. My sensitivity to them and their needs is stronger than even my craving for rest after a long, exhausting day.

Could it be that Jonah's ability to sleep through a storm—and perhaps our own inability to recognize the serious nature of our condition and consequences—is the result of a heart grown spiritually cold?

I'm not judging. I'm just saying.

Someone has written, "The hardening of a tender heart almost always starts with a justifiable action."[8] We think we know what we're doing. We consider our resistance toward God's plans and our lack of surrender to be minor compared to what others have done. We figure we do a lot of good things that ought to make up for our admitted weaknesses here and there, in one or two areas. We don't think God expects us to be so radical and on guard all the time. We've still got to have a life, right?

Those are the kinds of justifications that black out the windows, that keep us from seeing how far we've already stooped and how far down we could still plummet even from here. Those are the deceptive rationales the enemy spouts that deaden our spiritual awareness, causing us to lose our sense of direction and purpose, making us think we're cool with what's happening or at least holding steady, when in reality we're sinking like a rock, getting farther away every day from the person we think ourselves to be, the person we imagine as being pretty taut, pretty together. Before we know it, our senses are desensitized. We're sleeping right through the warnings, the signals, the stirring convictions, all the signs that tell us we're headed the wrong way.

Being asleep is how you end up staring at a half-empty bottle you said you were only going to take a sip of. Being asleep is how you end up halfway through the night with a guy you once said you'd never even go out with. Being asleep is how you end up doing things today that your personal sense of dignity would've never allowed you to do three years ago. But here you are. It's gotten this bad. Bad to worse.

Have you let yourself drift off to sleep, right here in the middle of life? Right when God is calling you to greater things? Right when other people need your encouragement and example the most? Right when the opportunity for pursuing significance is no more than one obedient choice away?

There is nothing pretty about the slippery slope of sin, disobedience, and resistance to God. Nothing nice that comes from running. Nothing sweet about the sleep of the spiritually seduced. The path downward possesses a gravity that becomes harder and harder to counteract the lower and lower you plunge.

Down is a direction that doesn't always feel panicky while we're on the descent, but it invariably leads to the bottom nonetheless. Whether we see it and know it, or whether we go there without really noticing, there's no escaping where it takes us.

Until we decide to look up.

— Going Up? —

My friend Holly Wagner, along with her husband, serves the Oasis Christian Center in Los Angeles, where she oversees the women's ministry of the church, better known as "GodChicks." But before Holly was so actively engaged in church leadership and discipleship, she was a Hollywood actress and talk-show host, successfully turning her dreams for stardom into real celebrity.

Her main openings had come in the nighttime soap-opera genre, where her beautiful looks and engaging character portrayals had placed her on the cover of national magazines as a rising up-and-comer. More movies and millions were in her future. At the young age of twenty-one, she was making it big in an industry that thousands of other girls just like her would give their right arm to crack.

But Holly was a believer in Jesus Christ. And the indwelling voice of the Holy Spirit was telling her these roles were not what He had saved and set her apart for. When new offers like these came calling in the future, she needed to learn a new word to speak in response—"No!"

Acting is an honorable art and profession. The issue in this particular case was not that Holly had pursued a California acting career to begin with but rather that God was intervening in her life at this moment in time, beginning to take her in another direction. Like with Jonah, the issue wasn't her work; it was her *willingness* to yield to God's will. If His plan had been for her to continue, fine. She could've kept on being obedient doing *that*. But because God was making no bones about drawing her away from a professional track that wasn't His unique purpose for her and her future, then ignoring or going around His instructions would have been rebellion toward Him. And Holly wasn't playing that role.

Not exactly what her talent agent wanted to hear. Not when he had big plans for his rising star and dollar signs in his eyes.

Because no sooner had she made her decision to steer away from less wholesome parts than Satan made sure she got an offer she couldn't refuse.

Holly had read for a part in another TV series, working from a partial script that didn't reveal in complete detail the direction this character would be taken or what exactly this show would be about. But when she asked for and took home the full script to review, she soon realized this was another questionable role she didn't want any piece of. She phoned her agent and told him she couldn't do it.

"But, Holly, I just got a callback for you on this audition. It's down to you and just a couple of others."

"Doesn't matter. I'm not doing it."

Against his wants and wishes and personal earning potential, Holly's talent rep dutifully made the call to the production company—(a *major* production company)—and apologized for his client's misgivings. To which they unexpectedly responded, "Tell her the part's hers."

Oh, great.

Back and forth this went. They really wanted her. She really wasn't budging. And yet the offer was not only repeatedly extended but was ultimately doubled. We're talking big bucks here! Her agent was starting to think her little hold-out strategy was *brilliant*.

"I'm not holding out," she told him. "Parts like these are not good for my soul! Don't you understand that?" But even her Christian friends couldn't understand it. Didn't Holly realize what a light for Christ she could be on the set of a dark, smutty soap opera? Didn't she know how many Bibles she could buy and ship to China with the money she'd be making?

Despite all of this, she'd made a decision. A first decision. And she was sticking with it. Despite all sorts of reasons and rationales, she was not going to let this take her down. She was rolling with God's intervention even if at times she felt like she might be making a mistake.

Today she spends her time talking about Jesus with women all over the country. She has a long, un-Hollywood-like marriage as well as two precious children. Even if the occasional "wonder what if" question may pop up out of nowhere, she doesn't regret one bit her decision to yield to the interruption, to take God up on His divine intervention. She feels that there is no comparison to what she's doing today—fully engaging in ministry to women, serving the church alongside her husband, spiritually investing in the lives of other actors who have walked a similar road—that comes anywhere close to what television acting could have done for her. Yes, she'd taken a personal stand of obedience to God's calling that eventually led her out of a lucrative acting career, but she knows for certain—for her—she'd be regretting it every minute today if she hadn't. An interruption? Not after all. This was indeed a divine intervention.

When life offered down, Holly chose up.

Jonah's life, on the other hand (as we're about to see), wasn't finished going south. And yours won't be either if you have other plans than following God wherever He tells you to go, trusting Him whatever He asks you to walk through, even if it just seems like one big interruption in your otherwise inviting, rosy path of living.

Down is always available—easy to get to but never easy to get out of—especially when (like Jonah) you're too knotted up within yourself to notice, when you've drifted off to sleep and don't realize the depths to which you've fallen.

CHAPTER 6

Wake-Up Call

*The LORD hurled a great wind on the sea and there was a
great storm on the sea so that the ship was about to break
up. . . . But Jonah had gone below into the hold of the ship,
lain down and fallen sound asleep.*

JONAH 1:4–5

Jonah may not have known it, but there is a worse place to be
than in a storm.

For him that place would have been Tarshish.

Let's just imagine for a second that this faraway region of the
ancient world was a rustic, woodsy setting with nice weather and
good fishing. Not a posh resort by any means but the kind of
place where a man could go to forget all his troubles, a million
miles away from worry and responsibility. An area that made up
for its lack of culture and amenities by providing lots of peace and
quiet—ample room to stretch your legs, plenty of space between
you and your nearest neighbor, a beautiful view of the moon and
stars at night.

Jonah had flipped through every page and panel of the Tarsh-ish travel brochures. Apparently he liked what he saw. And yet nowhere in this exotic destination was there a place where he could go to buy a certain commodity that had once been a reg-ular, trusted staple of his daily life. Even in the rebellious state of mind he was in as he boarded that ship, Jonah had to know from long experience as a prophet of God that if he made it to Tarshish, he would one day—not immediately, of course, but *one day*—yearn for something special he'd left behind in Jerusalem, something he'd miss not having in his old age.

If he had sailed into port at his new home away from home on the edge of the civilized world, Jonah would've likely spent his remaining years without ever again pulling the cloak of God's favor around his back, without ever again sensing the thrill or contentment of being part of God's plans, without ever experi-encing His manifest presence at the temple. How many mornings would he wake up over there and walk out into the sunshine—feeling the same golden rays that shone on his homeland a world away—and miss the warmth it used to bring him, not just to his face and shoulders but to his soul, to his spirit?

Have you ever fled to "Tarshish"—someplace that feels much more exciting and inviting than doing God's will? Ever decided you'd had enough of what God expected of you and were headed off to do what you wanted for a change? Ever decided to check out emotionally on your marriage and children and quit being burdened about whether or not everybody's getting what they need from you?

Doesn't keep you happy and laid-back for long, does it?

That's because no matter how remote and relaxing, noth-ing fills the void of abandoned purpose. Nothing feels the same anymore when you're running from God. The freedoms that appealed to Jonah most about Tarshish would eventually become empty promises, then worse—dark, heavy regrets that would mock him the rest of his life. Isn't that just Satan's way? Always? Jonah, sound asleep below deck, didn't fully realize this fact yet. But God certainly did.

And so God did something about it. He graciously refused to let Jonah's deep sleep prevent him from experiencing His will. He intervened.

And how!

We've all been in storms. And then we've all been in . . . *storms!* You know, the ones where the TV weather people are telling you to run and hide in your basement. The ones where the trash can lids blow off and rattle into the street. The ones where 1:00 in the afternoon looks like the middle of the night—lightning strikes, booming thunder, screaming winds, pouring rain. Jonah's storm came with that kind of fury . . . and then some.

> The LORD hurled a great wind on the sea and
> there was a great storm on the sea so that
> the ship was about to break up. (Jon. 1:4)

I'd call this an interruption *within* an interruption. God had already intervened in Jonah's life, inviting him to be involved in a mighty miracle of national repentance at Nineveh. And now—with Jonah thinking he'd pretty much put the kibosh on that—God intervened again. What had likely been tried as a gentle stirring in the prophet's spirit now came with thunder and lightning and the real prospect of shipwreck and death.

The perfect storm.

Because if not for *this* storm—at this particularly high level of volume and intensity—Jonah might've stayed below deck undisturbed all the way to his chosen getaway in Tarshish. God, however, couldn't bear to see this happen. Couldn't stand by while Jonah ruined his life. Couldn't remain silent while a precious child of the King took himself not only out of God's will but out from under God's blessing.

That's why He sent the storm. Not to *take* his life but to return it more fully to him.

Has that ever happened to you?

A man refuses to respond to a call of God—to leave his lucrative corporate job to involve himself in planting a local church. He's too afraid to commit, too unsure of what it all might mean. Then one Friday afternoon his boss calls him into his office, closes the door, and announces that due to budget cuts and slumping revenues, the company is having to take the unfortunate step of deleting a number of positions. One of them is his.

In blows the storm.

A young single woman is just about to accept a proposal, one she knows she shouldn't, but her heart can't seem to decline. Her best attempts at talking herself out of a relationship with this man—who is fantastic in so many ways but so wrong for her in all the ways that matter—are too weak to override what she's feeling. Then he shows up one day, not with a ring but with a revelation: there's another relationship he wants to pursue, and he thinks it's best if they take a little break for now.

In blows the storm.

A teenager balks at speaking a word of Christian challenge to a friend who's beginning to show signs of compromise in her personal life. She's not sure she should get involved. Doesn't know how the other person might take it. Then the phone rings late one night with news that this friend of hers has been in a car crash, taken to the hospital in an ambulance. How differently does she feel now, knowing she was hesitant to follow up on a nudge from the Holy Spirit? How is this loud crash of regret and confusion going to change the way she responds to Him in the future?

In blows the storm.

A middle-aged guy has known for years he should quit doing this, but he hasn't followed through. It's the one sin he's always justified to himself because of everything he's forced to put up with from his family, his past, and his other problems. To him, it's a reasonable escape. Yes, he knows it's wrong, but he's given in and learned to live with what it costs him as far as his relationship with God is concerned. It's his one little secret that comes to mind during Communion service, but on most other days of the year, it just comes *between* him and God—*between* him and unbroken fellowship. Then during a routine physical one October afternoon, his doctor walks into the examining room with a clipboard, a worried expression, and the number of a specialist for him to call about a concern that showed up in his bloodwork.

In blows the storm.

And thank God for it. Yes, I said it.

"Thank God for the storm."

Have you ever said those words? It's not a statement we'd ever expect to make. When we're in the midst of a crisis—when we're encountering the interruption within the interruption—the loss seems too severe, the pain is too strong, the setback feels too final and irreversible. It's all so terribly depressing. And yet God has certainly succeeded at getting our attention, hasn't He? Anything less turbulent might not have been enough, but now He's radically changed our perspective. And in the days and years that follow, we may look back with stunned relief at how close we came to sailing off the deep end . . . if not for His stormy intervention.

Jonah had been roused from his bunk by the captain during the storm—the stares of those roguish sailors peering down at him, telling him to get up and help them do something. The captain shouted,

> Get up, call on your god. Perhaps your god will be
> concerned about us so that we will not perish. (v. 6)

Think of it—a pagan ship commander calling a believer like Jonah to pray.

Isn't this much like what happens today when it takes the world to arouse the church—when their efforts for the hurting and needy put ours to shame, when their passions for certain causes and concerns outmatch the intensity of our own, even though we are bearers of the matchless gospel of Jesus Christ? Their eagerness to cry out for help beyond themselves when they find themselves in trouble, even in a generalized way toward a generalized god, should never rival our quickness to rush back into intimacy with our Father, who is truly able to help us in our times of greatest need—even when we've put our own lives into harm's way.

So you'd think at this point, embarrassed by the spiritual role reversal, Jonah would've come clean about who he was, where he was from, where he was going. Instead he sat silently through their nervous charade of casting lots, their crude way of determining who was to blame for this furious squall of nature. It wasn't until "the lot fell on Jonah" (v. 7) that he finally crumbled under their scrutiny and admitted the truth. I can't help but wonder if this prophet from Israel was a bit ashamed to speak the name of his God in conjunction with his own.

And yet look what the storm had done. Look at the tiny flicker of life emanating from Jonah's hardened heart and conscience as he declares, "I am a Hebrew, and I fear the LORD God of heaven who made the sea and the dry land" (v. 9). Sense the tiny ember of hope you feel that God might not be done with this guy after all.

If it hadn't been for our storms, that cause us to remember who and whose we are and where we are headed, we might not be here today. I wouldn't be writing this book. You might not have any interest in reading it. We'd be different people if our God had washed His hands of our situation and allowed us to keep wandering off in the direction of our first hunches and natural inclinations.

Yes, I thank God for His storms. They remind me who I really am. They remind me who my God really is.

—— Love on the Rocks ——

Not long ago I was standing in line at the grocery store, just doing the usual routine, transferring my things from cart to conveyor belt, when immediately behind me, in a tone that drew everyone's attention from all around, a young girl began back talking her mother in a most harsh and disrespectful way. I'm a simple Southern girl, OK? So forgive me if I still hold to the code of conduct that says honoring your parents applies to everything from Sunday manners to shopping trips. This little smarty-pants really got under my bonnet.

It wasn't the mother in me but just the fellow human being who wanted to spin around, grab that young lady's chin in my hand, squeeze her sassy lips a bit tightly, and tell her that giving an apology to her mom right now might—*might!*—convince me to let go and return to being a nice, generic stranger in the shopping line.

Actually, only one thing kept me from doing it: this girl wasn't my child. Lack of relationship made all the difference.

I'm sure you've watched other people getting away with all kinds of careless, self-absorbed behaviors. You've watched in astonishment as they've refused Christ as Savior, giving themselves over to sinful lifestyles without a seeming care that they might be doing something wrong.

Perhaps you've secretly wished you, too, could live with such a pleasure-based, unexamined attitude toward life. You've wondered why God seems so relentless in keeping the pressure on you, why every minor lack of surrender is met with biblical admonishment, why you can't just not care about being so spiritually responsible all the time, like when you're out to dinner, out of town, or otherwise off duty.

Well, there's a very good reason: because you're His child. And our Father disciplines His children (see Heb. 12:7). His involvement in your affairs is a revelation of His affection and relationship with you. And if you'll listen and respond to it, not only will you stop considering His correction a curse to be endured, but you'll see Him turn it into a *blessing* before He's through. The sight of storm clouds in your life is an indication of His love for you, His desire to see you steered back in the direction of His will. Because, let's face it, His will is always our best place to be—not free of challenge, necessarily, but free of those discouraging nights and weekends when we feel like we've wasted our lives on nothing. Being true to His purpose sets us up for a life of lasting meaning.

You may feel like God is spoiling your fun, but He's actually saving your skin. The worst thing in the world He could do to you (and me) is to do nothing while we're out there doing our dead-level best to get away from His will. So "do not fret because of evildoers, be not envious toward wrongdoers" (Ps. 37:1). He's on to you because you're His beloved.

If you have kids, you know exactly what I mean. When I see my children journeying away from the direction I know is best for them, the reason I bring a "storm" to bear on their lives is because I understand—much better than they do—that it's not *me* but rather the *behavior* they're displaying that's going to cause them the most problem in life. My discipline, which may seem heavy and oppressive to them at the moment, is actually their straightest shot to getting back on track. Without my intervention, their desire to run from teachability and obedience and brotherly kindness is just going to put them on a slow boat to Tarshish—a place that looks a whole lot better in the chamber of commerce ads than it turns out to be in real life.

I correct their course because they're mine. Because I know what they need most.

Because I love them.

And that's exactly why God treats us like He does. His storms that shake our lives are often disciplinary measures. When we're trailing away into sin, He's working hard to bring us back. When we're slipping off into error and bad judgment, He's adapting His teaching style to communicate in ways we're more likely to understand. When we're on the run from His presence, when we're refusing to yield our hearts to what He's asking of us, when we won't agree that His plans are a better alternative than ours, when we're snoozing all the way to Tarshish, He's not about to watch us stand perpetually outside His will, not when His abiding purposes are the only things that promise His kids freedom and real adventure and unspeakable joy. "For those whom the Lord loves He disciplines" (Heb. 12:6). It's not something to run from. It's something to be thankful for.

Remember the Disney movie *Monsters, Inc.*, where a wacky utility company powers their whole town by transforming children's screams into energy? Remember their motto? "We Scare Because We Care." God doesn't take delight in our pain, of course, but at the same time He's not above upsetting our apple cart if He knows we're about to drive it off the cliff.

If you had been walking around with me for much of my life, you'd have seen me caught out in a storm plenty of times— my clothes and hair all wet, my arms pressed down on top of my head, running for shelter as fast as my feet could carry me. No amount of sprinkles or springtime showers could have made me run so desperately for safety. Only a storm could do it. And my God has been faithful to spin them over my head more times than I can count.

If you're in a storm pattern right now, wake up! Look around and find your bearings again. Then, instead of shaking your fist toward the heavens, start thanking your gracious heavenly Father for loving you enough to make your slumber too uncomfortable for you to stay in.

You're His child. And He alone knows what's best for you.

—— Good Reasons for Rainy Seasons ——

I can't leave our meteorology discussion behind without bringing up something else.

The sailors on board the vessel with Jonah were most likely Phoenicians, pagans who came from a polytheistic culture. They worshipped a plethora of gods, each of which governed a different aspect of nature and was easily offended. So when trouble arose, like this savage storm on the Mediterranean, these men never knew *who* had done *what* to anger a particular deity. That's why "every man cried to his god" (v. 5) as the waves grew uncontrollable in an effort to make amends and tidy up any spiritual messes they may have unknowingly made.

Yet after Jonah had been exposed as the source of this monsoon and declared himself related to the one God "who made the sea" (v. 9) on which they were being tossed, these same grizzled sailors were not praying to their personal gods anymore but to the God of Jonah. From verses 14 to 16, they were addressing Him by the name Yahweh, the specific covenant name given to Israel.

This is incredibly noteworthy—pagan men recognizing the supremacy of this God of power, justice, and authority, as compared to the measly gods from whom they'd been crying for help before. As the first chapter of the book of Jonah nears its end, the

Scripture confirms that these men "feared the LORD greatly, and they offered a sacrifice to the LORD and made vows" (v. 16). Turns out Jonah's storm didn't just do *him* some good; it had a radically beneficial effect on others too. The thunderous rainstorm caused enough fear among the unbelieving to prepare them for a God encounter of their own.

Are you discouraged because of the storm your decisions may have caused others around you to endure? God is truly a multi-tasking whiz. He'll use the same storm that shivers our spiritual timbers to create changes in other people as well. Whether from watching our response or facing similar repercussions right along with us, they may discover their own opportunity to do business with God, the same way the storm formed the perfect backdrop for pagan mariners to encounter Him.

Yes, our Lord can get a lot done with a divine intervention. He will not allow fair weather to keep us from knowing Him, not just in a ceremonial way but in a serious, sensitive way—not just in a technically transacted way but in a real, responsive way. How often we throw our hands up in the air, beg for mercy, resent the interruption. But God wisely knows when only a storm will do, when no lighter form of inconvenience can alert us to who we really are and who He desires to be in us.

So wake up. Set your feet on the floor. Stand under the revealing shower of reality. Smell the clear-headed coffee of His Word and His truth.

Sometimes it just takes a storm to get us back to our senses, back to where we realize that no desire, distraction, or diversion can ever satisfy the deepest hungers of our souls. And your Father loves you too much not to send one.

Part 3

Repentance at Sea

CHAPTER 7

Now What?

*So they said to him, "What should we do to you that the
sea may become calm for us?"—for the sea was becoming
increasingly stormy.*

JONAH 1:11

So you're awake now.

And thank God for that.

Storm clouds came rumbling, tumbling, and thundering
through your life, packing enough force to pry open your heavy
spiritual eyelids. And it's pretty obvious to you now that you've
been running in the wrong direction. Hard to admit but nice to
know. So here you sit, blurry eyed and a bit stunned at how far off
the beaten path of God's direction you may have wandered. You
have one question on your mind . . .

Now what?

It's the question that hangs in the air after you've made a mistake or incurred a problem. It's the inquiry that swims around in
your mind when circumstances have gone haywire, when you're
in the midst of some horrid consequences brought about by your

rebellion. It's the query that begs an answer while we navigate this interrupted life.

What do I do next?

That's pretty much the same question the sailors had for Jonah.

Sure, Jonah was now awake and had 'fessed up. He'd said he was a Hebrew and that his God was the One who ruled the sea. But the storm still raged on—increasingly so! The ship still threatened to break into pieces. Their lives were still at stake. So with their hearts racing and their voices shaking, they yelled with fervor at Jonah over the noise of the tumultuous storm, "What should we do to you that the sea may become calm for us?" (Jon. 1:11).

The way Jonah responded to this question gives us incredible insight into the fundamentals of getting back on track, which is something we all need. Because we've all been there, haven't we? We've all been shocked to discover the mess we've made, the amount of running we've done, and the storm we've forced others to endure. We've all wanted to figure out how to get a bit of peace introduced into all this chaos, especially if it's the much more paralyzing kind that can ravage us inside whenever we've failed to follow God through a life interruption.

Know how it feels to be paralyzed by fear and guilt? Familiar with that stunned, disorienting sense of panic that seizes you when, after working like crazy to keep your skeletons locked in the closet, they all become suddenly, ruthlessly exposed? You feel dizzy. Desperate. Your chest aches. Your nerves tingle. You can hardly think about anything else. It wakes you up in the night—hanging right there, right over you. Immovable. Impossible. Then with your first rational thought of the morning, it's right back again, hungry for more. Eating you for breakfast.

Oh, sure, we can talk about how awful other people are, wondering how they live with themselves after doing some of the things they've done. But every time we wash our hands in the bathroom sink, we come face-to-face with a seasoned sinner. A runaway. One look at yourself—at *myself*—and we know we've been in Jonah's spot before. We know how intense the storm can get.

So . . . what now? What's the next move?

Jonah's pondering of this question compelled him to do something that many of us would like to try avoiding, and yet we *mustn't* avoid it if we ever hope to deboard from this boat ride that's taking us out of God's will. He stood surrounded by captain and crew below the heaving decks of the storm-tossed ship, and with his options for escape and anonymity dwindling down to none, he did one simple yet powerful thing. He said it was his fault. He owned responsibility. He told what he had done.

> The men knew that he was fleeing from the presence of
> the LORD, because he had told them. (Jon. 1:10)

Yes indeed, Jonah took ownership for the disobedience that had gotten them all in this mess in the first place, "for I know that on account of me this great storm has come upon you" (v. 12).

Guys, it's me.

Please don't race past this point without letting it settle in. I know, given the circumstances, Jonah's admission of guilt seemed to be about his only real option at the moment. But we've all been caught in situations where owning up is obviously the right thing to do. Does that always make us quick to admit that we're the one to blame?

Accepting blame is an enormous first step on the road of return—a "now what" step that anybody in Jonah's position *must* take—and yet this is where so many of us get tripped up.

A friend of mine was visiting here not long ago, and I decided to take her to a new restaurant I'd heard about in downtown Dallas. I called ahead to get directions, then did my best to navigate all the one-way streets that make our metroplex such an enjoyable driving experience. (I'm guessing there must have been a *huge* sale on "No Left Turn" signs when they were dreaming up this traffic pattern!) Still, I was doing all right until I got tangled up in a construction area, where some of the old familiar markers I was accustomed to seeing had been replaced by temporary signage. Add to that the maze of orange cones and caution tape, and before I knew what was happening, my lane veered back onto the freeway I had just exited a few minutes before to get here.

Our dinner was now *that* way, and we were going the other way. At sixty miles an hour.

Now what?

You know, it would've been nice if the guy I'd called for directions had told me to expect some delays and road confusion as I neared their parking lot. I could've blamed *him*. Might've been nice, too, if our city planners had given us the option of getting from Point A to Point B without always having to circle the next block. Could've just blamed *them*. But here I was by mistake, hungry and headed in the opposite direction. And even though I really wanted to eat at this one particular place, I was seriously starting to think about settling for any of several others I knew how to locate from here. After all, this wasn't my friend's hometown. She didn't need to know I was lost; and, I admit, I was a bit embarrassed to tell her.

What's your first tendency when you're caught in a mistake? Blame everybody else? Feel sorry for yourself? Settle for whatever you can salvage without further damaging your dignity? Try not to let anyone see you're at fault? Maybe not even allow yourself to come to grips with the fact that *you are*?

Imagine, for example—as writer and speaker Donna Otto shared with me one day—that you're in a hurry, waiting on an elevator to take you down to the lobby of your hotel. When the car finally arrives, it's incredibly full, and from the unspoken looks on the passengers' faces, you can tell they're hoping you'll wait for the next one. They can tell from yours, however, that you really need to hop on. Like, now!

So people start shifting their bodies toward the left, right, and back, cramming themselves together even more tightly to make room for one more. You're right in the middle, in front of everyone, your eyes facing outward into the hallway, with all other eyes focused annoyingly in your direction. The bell rings, the door closes, and the elevator finally begins to move.

Up.

Oh, great. You imposed on these people because you were in such a rush to get downstairs, and now you're heading twenty-two floors up, farther away every second from your desired destination. So there you stand, elbow to elbow with a crowd of strangers you've delayed and inconvenienced to the point of discomfort, knowing full well you need to stop and get off, yet you're frozen with humiliation. You've made a mistake. Now what do you do?

I'm sure we could pick a thousand of these scenarios and illustrations. Each one would leave behind its own little lesson and set of questions. But the one that really matters is the real-life story that comes with your own name and circumstance painted on it, a time when you've come face-to-face with your running, when all your avenues for evasion have been sealed off and boarded up, when every finger of accusation (even the one attached to your own hand) is pointing your direction, leaving you nowhere else to turn. You're caught red-handed, dead to rights. And unless you want things to get worse with no hopes of getting any better, you need to make a courageous choice.

So . . . will you?

Like Jonah, perhaps you've been sailing along, hoping to ride out these consequences, but now your cover's been blown, and you're forced to deal with this thing. You can be too embarrassed to deal with it. You can try justifying your way out of it. You can blame someone else for it. You can live under a heaping pile of guilt for the rest of your life about it.

Or how's this—you can just acknowledge you've messed up and get on with it. Accepting blame is always the first right step in the progression of repentance.

And if you don't think you can do that, there's Someone here who can help.

—— Any Questions? ——

A lot of questions were being shouted at Jonah over the roar of the tempest and the howls of his shipmates.

> Tell us, now! On whose account has this calamity
> struck us? What is your occupation? And where
> do you come from? What is your country?
> From what people are you? (Jon. 1:8)

Five questions, like weighty boulders, all being hurled at him in quick succession. He probably felt pummeled under the burden of interrogation. Probably couldn't even think fast enough to take them all in, to hear everything these men were asking for, much less to feed them the answers they were wanting so ravenously.

Yet, no doubt, the significance of these questions penetrated Jonah's heart and head. The reality of who he was, where he was from, and what he was doing must have felt like a searing weight on his rebellious conscience as the truth began dawning on him again. He could only muster enough courage to whisper from the depths of his weakened, anxious soul, "I am a Hebrew, and I fear the LORD God of heaven" (v. 9).

Not exactly a confession yet. Or was it?

According to scholars this description he chose for himself—"a Hebrew"—was more than a simple declaration of nationality. It was a word "commonly used to distinguish the people of God from those of other nations."[9] In fact, even Gentiles would often use this term as a way of differentiating between themselves and those who served Yahweh, those who were the beneficiaries of covenantal relationship with Him. So in declaring himself a Hebrew, Jonah couldn't help but be reminded of his connection to the one true God. This seemed to cause the ministry of God's Spirit to wash over him. His heart was overwhelmed with conviction, and he could do nothing less than proceed to spill out a laundry list of adjectives to describe the God who governs His people—the God who governed this runaway prophet, even on the sea-lane to Tarshish.

"I fear the LORD . . ."

". . . the LORD God . . ."

". . . the LORD God of heaven . . ."

The God who made the sea.

Oh, and the dry land too.

This is a vital development. It's reminiscent of David's classic confession from Psalm 51, as he tried coming to grips with his adulterous guilt, crying out to God:

> Against You, You only, I have sinned and done
> what is evil in Your sight, so that You are justified
> when You speak and blameless when You judge." (v. 4)

This was not merely some prepared statement for David to read at a hastily called press conference, officially announcing his apology. He didn't care if the public found him to be genuinely remorseful. David's issue was not with other people's disappointment and hard questions but with God, the One he had primarily offended. The Lord's searchlight of truth had been what finally got through to his heavily clouded heart.

And though Jonah may not have been fully remorseful yet (it's clear from Jonah 4:2 that he was still hoping Nineveh would be destroyed), a divine storm had begun raging within him, even while the storm outside continued to rage on at sea. His journey out of danger was far, far from over. But be sure of this: *it had begun*. The change in Jonah's path from the road of rebellion to the pathway of penitence was underway.

And it all began with those first piercing questions.

Are you listening? Do you hear God's Spirit raising questions deep within you? Are there a few divine inquiries swimming around in your heart that seem to pop up at the oddest times— while you're stuck in traffic, cooking dinner, folding clothes, having a meeting? Are they dredging up some revealing answers about where you are and what you've been doing? Is He making it quite clear that what you've been hiding from others—perhaps even hiding from yourself—is not hidden at all before "the eyes of Him with whom we have to do" (Heb. 4:13)?

Don't ignore the Spirit's attempts to engage you, my friend. The conviction, the stirring, is the call of your Father, drawing you back to Himself, inviting you to put an end to your running, to start what needs to happen for things to get turned back around. Answer these—submit to these—and you'll be on the right track to healing and wholeness.

—— Whatever the Cost ——

Jonah heard the questions. He admitted he'd been running and was willing to take the blame for his decision. Now it was time for the next step of repentance—just as it is for us when we've resisted God's invitation to follow Him through an interruption. *Accepting God's loving discipline* is how the sin you've admitted and acknowledged becomes the sin you're actually beginning to repent of. It means you're not just aware that you've done wrong; you're also aware that you need His help to keep you from going back, from ever deciding that running is a better option than obedience.

By the time the sailors got around to tossing Jonah overboard, they'd become fairly indiscriminate about what they were choosing to part with. "Precious metals, horses and mules, ivory and various other products" had already been tossed.[10] Few things were deemed worth saving with their lives so perilously at stake. The only line they appeared unwilling to cross, in terms of what they were inclined to abandon to the furious waters . . . was Jonah. Even pagan mariners apparently understand the concept of having a check in their spirit.

Yet, funny thing, Jonah was offering. That's what makes their hesitance a little harder to understand. Because, look, if it was me—if I'd seen some overzealous shipmates coming my direction, looking like I might be the next thing going overboard—they'd have been chasing me up one side and down the other of that sloshy deck. I mean, I enjoy swimming with the kids, and I've ridden in a boat or two in my time, but I don't have any desire to be thrown overboard. Even if they'd been able to corral me by force, I'd have made sure they earned those black eye patches before we got anywhere near the edge.

But Jonah—how could he be so resigned to certain death? Why was he advising them to "pick me up and throw me into the sea" (Jon. 1:12), without even appearing to put up a struggle?

All I can figure is that Jonah was starting to learn experientially what he already knew deep down. He couldn't escape God. Couldn't run hard enough, fast enough, or far enough to get away. Couldn't just stop being His child anymore, His precious possession.

Again, I don't know if Jonah's repentance was truly reaching his core or not—(he never actually confesses any specific sin)—but let's admit, this is a much more surrendered, much more submitted prophet than we met at the beginning. Where he had once been unwilling to cede another ten minutes to discuss God's plans for him in Nineveh, now he seemed willing to yield his life to the Lord's righteous discipline. He was holding nothing back, not even a terrifying plunge into the dark, churning waters of the Mediterranean. In fact, if the sailors hadn't done it for him, you get the feeling he might've hurled himself into the deep if he thought the sacrifice would put himself and these poor men out of their misery.

God now had what He wanted in the first place—a prophet willing to listen and obey, a servant ready to take responsibility for his calling, a man who might even yet have a bit of ministry left in store for him.

When Jerry and I discipline our sons, we're after a heart change, not just a change in their behavior. If I send one of the boys to his room for a while, I'm hoping he'll use the time to consider his actions, think how he's affected others, and determine what he could've done differently. I want him to emerge not just with an apology but with a heart that's ready to do something about it. I'm not eager to make him a good kid for the afternoon but rather an upstanding young man for the rest of his lifetime.

As a parent, I'm hoping that discipline will affect his heart, softening him, keeping this from being just an isolated episode that won't have any lasting effect. I'm not after a temporary blip on his behavioral radar screen. If that's the extent of it, the day will end, and we'll start again, but count on it—we'll be back here before long.

Yaweh was after Jonah's heart and He's after ours as well.

Accepting discipline can be difficult. Truth is, this whole business of repentance can be hard. The experience of being caught red-handed in the middle of your running can often be a miserably stormy ordeal to go through, one you might rather like to avoid altogether. But in trying to determine what to do next, Jonah's actions encourage us to do this: *acknowledge the sin* and *accept the discipline*. Turn yourself in to the authority of God's truth and justice, and see where the Lord chooses to take you from there.

Of course, it doesn't always mean that things will get better before they get worse. Repentance can feel bad even when it's working. That next step can still be a doozy.

But at least you can know it's a step in the right direction.

Repentance always is.

CHAPTER 8

A Fish Called Grace

And the LORD appointed a great fish to swallow Jonah, and Jonah was in the stomach of the fish three days and three nights.

JONAH 1:17

If you're trying this at home, you may want to move over to the kitchen sink or kneel down by the bathtub, or at least spread out some towels to catch the spills. I know it's a little messy, but we've come this far with Jonah, and I don't think any of us expected to make it through without getting a little wet, so . . .

Here goes.

First you'll need to get a regular-sized drinking glass, filled with water. You'll also need one other person to help you. But that's it. This is obviously something you can duplicate by using items that are already lying around your house (like your spouse, perhaps).

Now with the water glass in hand, stretch out your arm directly in front of you. No need to hold it perfectly straight, with elbow unbent, unless maybe you're needing to do a little toning work on your triceps. Eight-ounce weights are better than nothing.

When you feel like you're set, tell the lab partner you've enlisted to start shaking your arm—at whatever level of strength and force he or she chooses to apply. Meanwhile, you hold on and try to keep yourself as stable as you can. Now what do you expect to happen? Whether with violent movements or even gentle agitations, you'd anticipate seeing some water start sloshing over the rim of your glass and onto the ground. Pretty simple, right?

But now for the somewhat more difficult part: the explanation. *Why is the water spilling out?*

Of course, you know I'm not looking for the most readily apparent answer. Anybody might tell you that the reason water is pouring out is because someone's shaking your arm. But actually the person who's jostling you, making it hard for you to hold the glass steady, is merely a catalyst in this experiment. True, their role is definitely involved in the outcome, but it's not the primary reason you're getting this result. They could be shaking your arm *without* causing water to splash out if—what?—if you weren't holding something to spill.

The main reason water comes out of your glass is because water is in the glass.

It's the same reason we so often react to life interruptions with anger, rage, bitterness, panic, distrust, uncertainty, fear, touchiness, and a hundred other toxic contaminants. These things don't spill out of us merely because we're under a heavy stress load. We're not being forced by external pressures to operate out of character, not to be ourselves. Problems and tight spots are not what make us act in such shocking ways—complaining more than usual, arguing more than usual, turning into a person we hardly recognize.

No, all these wicked things are already inside us—hiding out, undetected, lying dormant until a sufficient level of shaking is able to jar them loose. Interruptions don't create them; they just expose them.

See, we think we get mad because a parent, a sibling, a spouse, a child, or a slow driver camped in the passing lane is causing us to act that way. The truth is, these irritations and interruptions are merely the catalyst that unclogs those stubborn nests of self-centeredness that have burrowed down deep within us.

We think the reason we melt into a quivering puddle of worry is because we have so much to carry, so many decisions to make, so many risks to manage, so many people to care for, so many plates to juggle, so many disappointments to get over. But frankly, these multiple responsibilities and challenges are simply agents that help us see we're still inclined to choose fretting over faith, no matter how much we say our trust is in the Lord.

We think we've grown fairly immune to pride and self-importance because of the knocks we've taken the last few years. But then someone else's confidence in our abilities turns into a new opportunity, an increased role in decision making, a position of leadership that draws the kinds of compliments we love hearing about ourselves, and suddenly those same old temperaments come roaring back in again, raising their ugly heads. Yes, even successes in our business, with our children, or in our ministry can uncover pride, envy, or other issues we may have unknowingly tucked away.

So these can be either negative or positive. Cash shortages. Job offers. Marital tension. Even a marriage proposal. Sometimes these are just the divine mechanisms God employs (or allows) to help us notice how much junk is still festering inside. Things we didn't know were there. Weaknesses that are sure to bite us hard later if they're not dealt with now while there's still time to replace and transform them, before they turn into habits so ingrained and impenetrable that they become our lifestyles.

This is not God's way to condemn us but only to change us. Laying bare our sins, secret fears, self-sufficiency, and insecurities is not an attempt to hurt us but only to help us. Odd as it may seem, this is actually a rescue operation, even if right now it feels like a real bear to put up with.

Or maybe like a giant fish with a man-sized appetite.

Call it terrifying.

Call it impossibly hard.

Call it ungodly, unfair, uncalled for.

Or why not just call it Grace?

—— Grace under Pressure ——

Jonah would have died, you know? Sure, three miserable days in a reeking aquarium of consequences must have scared the poor guy to death. At the time it may have seemed to him as though nothing could be worse than being buried alive in a fish's belly. But we can honestly say that if not for this big boy coming along when he did, Jonah would've died in the open water. He wouldn't have lived to see another day.

So this fish, as it turns out, had a name.

It was a fish called Grace.

When I get to heaven, I'm going to corner Jonah like an unashamed groupie who hangs around backstage after hours. I'm going to run up to him with a sackful of investigative questions, starting with the one they always ask people when outrageous things happen to them or a big news story breaks: "How did it feel?" We all want to know what it was really like to be caught in the middle of a tense, dramatic moment. What did you hear?

When did you realize you were in trouble? What went through your mind?

I guess we all wonder those same things about Jonah. How did he feel when he was flung from the boat by the rugged arms of his shipmates, when his body hit the roaring, raging waters of the sea? I'm sure he was prepared to drown (as prepared as a person can *ever* be)—losing the strength to stay afloat, aching for air but unable to catch a breath.

How long was he out there? Was he clear-headed enough to see that the storm had miraculously lifted, just like he'd said it would to the fearful crew on board the ship? Did he notice the mammoth sea creature approaching? Was he even aware of what was happening when it gobbled him up?

Wonder if he knew where he was when he found himself alive—not in the water any longer but definitely not in a place like anywhere else he'd ever been before. Between bouts of consciousness, with all those slimy textures and ghastly smells assaulting his senses and grossing him out, did he hunt for a way of escape? Did he locate a spot in that darkened digestive passage where he could sit down and lean back on something—some *icky* something? Did the horror of this place, coupled with the slow, maddening wait for death, cause him to deal with his regrets, making him think about all the stuff God had shaken out of him in the last few days?

I wonder.

You can almost feel sorry for him now, can't you? You can sort of imagine how this pitch-black prison illuminated his past mistakes in all their stark, haunting reality, making it hurt for him to look at. Perhaps, quite honestly, he hadn't fully realized at the time how serious an offense it had been to resist God's call to Nineveh. Sometimes it takes something as dire and dramatic as getting caught in a fish's belly to bring the gravity of our decisions to light.

It's a registered letter from the IRS, declaring that your tax return has been pulled for auditing—and you know you overstated your deductions by a good $10,000.

Caught.

It's the text message your spouse found on your cell phone that disclosed the secret sin you'd been hiding—maybe a touchy-feely, flirtatious relationship you've never been willing to put the brakes on.

Caught.

It's being told over lunch by a caring, concerned friend that she's noticed a real harshness and bitterness about you that wasn't there before. She just wonders if something's wrong you haven't told her. You really thought you'd done a better job of covering it.

Caught.

It's the ugly e-mail that accidentally gets routed to the person you made the snide comment about.

Caught.

It's the lie you told to avoid keeping a commitment, before being spotted somewhere doing something else.

Caught.

It's the fish's belly God appoints for his beloved "Jonahs." Oh, the panic, the shame, the heart-racing reality when you're caught red-handed. You feel like you're not going to make it through this now that everything's out in the open, now that everything's come undone.

On the contrary, my friend, you're going to make it through this drama specifically *because* everything's come undone. This fish is designed to keep you from going under once and for all. Had God not allowed you to get caught, you would've eventually drowned for sure. But this uncomfortable outcome He's allowed is giving you a chance to catch your breath, come to your senses, and become more completely His.

It turns out, a fish's belly is really a conducive place for someone to take all the time needed to get all these things straightened out. Enough time even for repentance to occur. It certainly was for Jonah.

> Jonah prayed to the Lord his God
> from the stomach of the fish. (Jon. 2:1)

He had started this process while on board the ship—*acknowledging his sin*. With the storm at full tilt, he had been willing to let the sailors toss him overboard—*accepting his discipline*. And now, with all hopes of running from God drained from his system, Jonah was being given the opportunity to take the next step in his repentance progression—*asking forgiveness*.

Did he take it? Not really. He never explicitly asked forgiveness. But while Jonah may not have fully realized the gravity of his disobedience, we can still say he was generally penitent. He realized he'd been miraculously spared, and this was his chance to get things right. So through his story you and I can still learn some critical lessons about true repentance and its effects on us. This is your chance, my friend. Right now, while you're trapped in the belly of your less than desirable circumstances, you can do business with God. In fact, it's for this reason He's preserved you.

Granted, we may only be able to hazard a guess at what Jonah's harrowing experience was like in the gullet of that great beast, but we know what it's like to be in a position where the only words left inside us to utter are prayers. Our situations may not have come with the same sights, sounds, and stenches as Jonah went through, but hasn't each of us sat surrounded by the repercussions of our callous, cowardly actions, forced to contemplate what we've done—in all its horrid detail?

This appointed consequence is just what we needed.

If Jonah was consciously aware of the fish's arrival and presence, if he was able to see it coming and drawing closer, to see that fish coming, he must have surely thought death was imminent. But what seems like it's been designed to kill us may actually be God's way of preserving us, rescuing us from what could be a far more dire consequence. Maybe, just maybe, the more vast the consequences we face, the more vast the work He plans to perform through us after it eases up or passes. When we feel His correction particularly heavy upon us, it's sometimes not so much in proportion to past or recent sin as in proportion to the great task awaiting us when He's done, when we've endured it.

I love the way pastor John Piper says it: "Adversity is redemptive; it is not merely punitive."[11] God isn't out to hurt you; He's out to redeem you. He's out to get you back to your senses, back to where you realize you've been headed the wrong direction, back where you're desperate to turn this misstep around if given the opportunity. Back to a place where you want His forgiveness as badly as you wanted your independence, where you crave accountability the way you used to crave your freedom, where the things you once cherished about your life with Him become the things you now desire more than life itself.

See, if you're a child of God, then the frustration, impatience, anger, and all those other things your interruption has purged to the surface are not the only occupants living inside your heart. You also house the indwelling Holy Spirit, who continually seeks the things of God even when you're not particularly wanting to. So just as trials and interruptions are capable of exposing the resistant tendencies and temperaments that still hang out in your life, they can also mark the moment when something else bubbles to the surface—your deep sense of need for God's deliverance, your too long forgotten fondness for the Father.

Sometimes it just takes a fish called Grace to reel it out of you.

—— Up from the Grave ——

If there was anything for Jonah to celebrate while he sat in the belly of the fish, it was this:

> I called out of my distress to the LORD,
> and He answered me. I cried for help from
> the depth of Sheol; You heard my voice. (Jon. 2:2)

God heard him. And God answered him.

What an overwhelming peace must have shrouded the rebellious prophet, even while he was cowering in despair in the middle of nowhere. To know that he was indeed not alone—that he was being heard by the One he'd been running from—must've felt like a trapped miner hearing his rescuers stamping into the shaft with the clank of pulleys, chains, and flashlights.

Our little one-year-old Jude was in the kitchen with me the other day while I was getting a little work done. He had crawled around behind a couple of nook stools that are positioned by our breakfast area and was playing there on the floor, just entertaining himself. But as his attention span waned and he was deciding to pack up his imagination and take it somewhere else, he found himself in a bit of a jam.

Without realizing it, he had worked his little body in between the wooden slats of one of the stools and had gotten sort of stuck. Couldn't go under it, couldn't go over it, couldn't go around it—you know, sometimes you get the bear, sometimes the bear gets you.

This bear had Jude.

I could see, of course, that he was struggling, trying to navigate himself out of the trap he'd fallen into. And the thought suddenly struck me, "Wow, this would be a perfect time for me to go brush my teeth." (My, how a mother's perspective changes from the first child to the third!) Yup, left him there where I knew he'd stay put for the minute it was going to take me to get the job done. He called out to me for a few seconds until he got busy with his toys under there again, and I completely ignored him, taking complete advantage of the makeshift playpen he'd unknowingly created for himself.

I'm so glad God is not like that—not with *any* of His children. The struggles you're facing, the fish you're sitting in while trying to work yourself through a season of repentance, are not going unnoticed. He hasn't slipped out on you to take care of other pressing matters, figuring you'll probably be fine until He can get back to check on you.

He's right here—right in there with you.

And He will not ignore your call for help.

I'll be honest, I almost get butterflies in my stomach when I see our old pal Jonah, desperately ill and out of sorts in this impossible snare of a consequence, praying "to the LORD his God from the stomach of the fish" (v. 1). As far as we can tell, praying is not something he had done since we first met him pulling out of Jerusalem on his way to Joppa. Throughout the whole storm sequence of chapter 1, everybody is praying *except* Jonah. In chapter 2, every single word of Jonah's is a prayer.

There's something about forgoing the privilege of prayer that almost always leads us into the fish's belly. And yet being in the fish's belly is bound to lead us back to it. In fact, I'm convinced that's one of the main things it's designed to do.

But if we aren't careful, we can allow it to have the opposite effect. Whether from the extraordinary discomfort, the overwhelming shame, the hopeless frustration, or any combination of emotions, we face the cruel temptation to hole up in our hardship and consider ourselves abandoned. Forgotten. Unforgiven. Unforgiveable.

Yet here we see Jonah—a spiritual leader of Israel who had hightailed it to Tarshish in front of God and everybody (as well as endless generations of Bible readers)—seizing on this opportunity to do business with God, to turn and look into His face from the thick darkness of his current condition, to cry out to Him in the midst of his despair, knowing that the Lord was his only hope of rescue. He could have resigned himself to this fate, and yet he didn't. He chose to cry out to the Lord "from the stomach of the fish" (v. 1).

No better place than here. No better time than now.

If you've been there—if you *are* there—hear God's Word to you today.

> The LORD longs to be gracious to you,
> and therefore He waits on high to have compassion on
> you. For the LORD is a God of justice; how blessed are all
> those who long for Him. (Isa. 30:18)

While His tough-loving discipline may have been required to help you recognize the extent of your running or to spotlight the place where you blocked Him from working in your life, repentance and restoration are near. Christ has won the right to declare you approved and acceptable in the eyes of the Father—as usable as ever—now that you've *acknowledged your fault, accepted your discipline,* and *asked forgiveness.* A forgiven sinner is always welcome at the throne of God.

A place called Grace.

If you've been running from God and you know it, if you've brought some consequences on yourself that are painful to endure, if you've caused others to suffer for your failure to live in full surrender to God's will and way, you can still call out to Him. You can seek a sure reconciliation with the One you've offended.

Jonah didn't confess his specific sins while he was crying out to God from the inside of his consequences. Time would tell whether or not he was through with the bad attitudes and deci-sions that had led him into such a trapped, confined space. He seemed to be agreeing with God about a lot of things—and was certainly sorry he'd been caught, of course—but it's hard to tell whether or not he was totally dismissing the argument that he'd been somewhat justified in doing what he did.

For us, however, the fish's belly can be the place where we lay aside our resistance to God's divine interventions for good, where we come clean about the selfish habits, the stubborn preferences, and the old running shoes we've allowed to clutter up the closet in our hearts and lives. We can be assured that when we "confess our sins, He is faithful and righteous to forgive us our sins and to cleanse us from all unrighteousness" (1 John 1:9).

Now let me be clear: doing all of this doesn't mean every-thing's necessarily going to change overnight. Jonah still had three days inside Moby Dick to sit and learn some things before God knew it was time for his circumstances to change. But we can gather from the prophetic foreshadowing of this event in rela-tion to Christ (who spent a similar three days in the darkness of death before emerging victoriously resurrected) that your release from this intense season of discipline will be at the precise, per-fect moment when God knows all has been accomplished in this season of your life. And even if some of your consequences con-tinue to linger, perhaps throughout the remainder of your life-time, it will not be to shame you but to be a testimony to others of your redemption, keeping you from wanting to go back again, protecting you from the fickle forgetfulness that too often resides in all of us.

God has brought you here to redeem you, my friend, not to destroy you. And your restoration and renewal need not wait another second.

Like Jonah, call out to Him for help in your distress. Cry out knowing that He hears you "from the depth of Sheol" (Jon. 2:2). Be confident that your prayer is reaching His "holy temple," even when you feel like you're "fainting away" (v. 7). Pray believing that God in His grace and mercy is going to bring your life up "from the pit" (v. 6)—not if, but when—despite the fact you may have dug this hole with your own rusty garden equipment.

I don't care how rote or clichéd or even nonexistent your prayer life has become, the fish's belly is your green light to turn it loose again with purpose and passion. Don't hold back.

If we learn anything from Jonah's experience in the ocean depths, it's that arduous, heartfelt, all-consuming prayer marks the heart of one who is learning the lessons of the fish's belly—one who's sailing past pride and selfishness and poor decision making on his way to a better place.

A place called Hope, in a fish called Grace.

— The Leftover Makeover —

Every Sunday growing up, I remember my mom cooking an extravagant meal. Sunday dinner. If I close my eyes, I can almost still smell it. Maybe a pot roast that had been cooking overnight, tender and juicy, or a fried chicken with golden brown skin and succulent spices. Full serving bowls of steaming hot vegetables, spooned onto our plates alongside a buttery slice of her home-made rolls and pumpkin bread. I could go on, but I know I'm making you hungry, and we're so close to finishing this chapter.

I don't know how she pulled it off. I try to duplicate her success with my own family, but it never seems to have that magical something she was able to add. Perhaps it's just the nostalgia of childhood that keeps it out of reach, but I do the best I can, and nobody seems to be suffering from malnutrition. My boys are growing bigger everyday, and the rest of us are . . . well, we're doing just fine, thank you.

But more than my amazement at how Mom concocted such incredible dinners Sunday after Sunday was the way she set the table on the following Monday or Tuesday, using bits and pieces left over from our big weekend meal. She would pull storage dishes from the refrigerator, peel off the plastic wrap, slicing and dicing as she went. Then she'd pour everything into a casserole dish, assemble it neatly and evenly along the bottom, pour some cream-of-something soup over the top, and finally sprinkle on a coating of shredded cheese. After forty-five minutes under foil at 350 degrees, she'd take it from the oven, ascribe it a stylish French-sounding name, and—*voilà!*

What my mom could do with leftovers.

But no one can do what God can—take the messes we've made, the problems we've caused, and rebuild them into something that looks suprisingly promising. He pours the cream of His Spirit over everything, sprinkles some grace and mercy on top, puts it in a hot oven of trial and adversity, and—*voilà!*—a delicious offering we never thought our lives would ever produce again, ready to serve to a hungry world that's equally in need of redemption.

This appetizing aroma wafting from the kitchen is one you can enjoy again, my friend, no matter what you've done up till now to stink up the place. Your Father is as willing and able as ever to turn your mistakes into miracles, salvaging what you thought was lost and devoid of any use. But no one's enjoying anything until you confess your running and rebellion and agree with God concerning what He's revealing about you. Until you ask forgiveness.

Until you truly repent.

So let the shaking begin. And whatever starts to spill out of the glass, thank the Lord He is purging you of poisons that would've continued to rob you of spiritual health, freedom, and abundance long into the future, stealing more from you than they already have. If you notice yourself showing surprising amounts of anger and discord as a result, or perhaps an insatiable appetite for sinful escapes, recognize you're seeing the hard-working results of God's faithful discipline in action, bringing even your hidden faults out into the open.

Beg for deliverance from these holdouts of your fallen human nature. Bravely cooperate with Him in standing strong, knowing how persistently these long-held tendencies try to reattach. And ask His forgiveness as He reveals them to you. Confess your need and inability to do anything about them without His help and empowerment. Want His healing and renewed usefulness as badly as you want out of this uncomfortable situation. And be ready to face your next interruption with a different kind of heart and mind-set.

There's a lot He can do in you . . . in a fish called Grace.

CHAPTER 9

Making Change

But I will sacrifice to You with the voice of thanksgiving.
That which I have vowed I will pay. Salvation is from the
LORD.

JONAH 2:9

One of my favorite television programs is *Clean House* on the Style Network. Ever seen it? They locate a family or couple whose household clutter has pretty much overtaken their ability to function. Then the zany host and her team swoop in to help them tackle their heaping load of challenges.

While a handyman builds new shelves to store all the things that are currently strewn haphazardly across the floor and furniture, a decorator begins sorting through whatever he can find to incorporate into a new overall design scheme. A professional organizer sifts through mounds of papers and supplies to figure out the best way to systematize the family's chaos, while a yard sale expert hunts for stuff to sell on the front lawn. Each half-hour episode captures the enormity of the task and makes it highly entertaining to watch, even though it looks like a nightmare to actually do.

During the final minutes of each telecast, the owners return home, surprised to find their familiar rooms and corners completely organized, gorgeously decorated, and squeaky-clean, rid of all the debilitating junk and disorder that once weighed the place down. Some laugh in utter amazement when they see it. Others cry. But every single one of them is always stunned beyond belief to see the transformation that's occurred in the short time they've been gone. What had seemed so impossible to overcome has now been restored to manageability and freedom.

They feel like they've gotten their lives back.

The host never leaves these excited people behind, however, without addressing the amount of upkeep required to maintain all the work that's been done. Those neat, tidy living surfaces won't keep themselves picked up on their own. Those nice, new drawers and cabinets won't stay carefully categorized without deliberate attention to detail. She explains to the family that her team is now leaving, and the responsibility for keeping this house a livable home is up to the people who actually live there. No more hoarding. No more buying things they don't need and stacking them in places where no one can walk. No more leaving things a mess and assuming somebody else will take care of it. If they want their house to stay clean, organized, and comfortable for friends and guests, they must make some changes to the way they operate.

They must choose to live differently.

And the same could be said for every one of us, as far as our personal lives are concerned. Just because we've *acknowledged our sin, accepted our discipline,* and *asked God's forgiveness,* the greatest blessings of repentance will continue to linger out there unrealized and beyond our grasp if—even after all of that, after doing all three of those things so well—we just end up going back to our old ways of living. What a shame to waste even a short season in the fish's belly without changing what got us there in the first place. Repentance requires walking down a different path, cooperating with God's Spirit to maintain what He has been working so hard to drain out of us.

We cannot stop at merely knowing and agreeing with God that we've taken a turn in the wrong direction. We must now *act in conjunction with God's direction.* Repentance is four-wheel drive.

Remember my silly experience trying to take my friend to a downtown restaurant, where we got turned around in a construction zone and ended up sailing back onto the freeway? It wouldn't have done me much good if all I did was admit that I was going the wrong way. Or just accepted the fact that I had cost myself some time and inconvenience. Or did nothing more than ask my friend to forgive me for not watching where I was going. The more time I wasted being sorry about what I'd done without doing anything to correct it, the farther and faster I sped away from the place I needed to be.

Repentance means getting off at the first exit on the road out of town, turning the car around as quickly as possible, and steering ourselves onto the road coming back.

For Jonah, it meant putting Tarshish in his rearview mirror. And getting Nineveh out of his blind spot.

— Out with the Old —

After being deposited back on dry land, Jonah both recalled and recorded the words he remembered from his distraught, desperate prayer. Judging from what he prayed in chapter 2, he obviously recognized the depths to which he had sunk, both physically and spiritually.

> For You had cast me into the deep, into the heart
> of the seas, and the current engulfed me. All
> Your breakers and billows passed over me. So I said,
> "I have been expelled from Your sight.". . . Water
> encompassed me to the point of death. The great
> deep engulfed me, weeds were wrapped around my
> head. I descended to the roots of the mountains. The
> earth with its bars was around me forever. (vv. 3–6)

He knew this was bad and that he had messed up royally. His experience inside the big fish had been a major reality check. Such experiences usually are.

But it needed to be much more than that. And for Jonah, it was. We can generally say that Yahweh's efforts at preserving and protecting Jonah's life in the fish's belly achieved the desired effect because he emerged from this shocking ordeal with more than just a past-tense awareness of how wrong he'd been. He also came to a clear understanding that he needed to make a change. Where he had once talked himself into running away from God, now he was already making prayerful plans to abandon the path of disobedience and defiance and get back in step with God's program.

His penitent prayer reveals that he was changing course.

He was going God's direction.

He planned to fulfill his calling.

Even if it wasn't really what he felt like doing.

And just for the record . . . it wasn't.

Jonah hadn't suddenly developed a strong interest and desire in going to Nineveh, even though he knew for sure he didn't want any more of God's swimming lessons. The fourth chapter of Jonah—postrevival (which we'll get to eventually)—reveals that he was still hoping the Ninevites didn't actually receive God's mercy. But nonetheless, he was *going*. Even while continuing to feel some fairly strong animosity toward his enemies, some lingering anger at ever being called away from Jerusalem in the first place, and probably an ongoing level of disappointment and disillusionment with God, Jonah was preparing to do the right thing.

That encourages me. One of the main reasons we so often try to drive repentance on three wheels is because we don't *feel* like changing the fourth one. Making the kinds of adjustments God is calling us to execute can leave us feeling a little . . . flat. We know we should turn from our chosen exit strategy and embrace our divine intervention. We're aware that we should go to Nineveh. We know that, but we're not exactly looking forward to *doing* that. And until we feel differently about it, how are we supposed to get our repentance shifted out of park?

Jonah illustrates for us that even when you don't feel like it, you can still make up your mind to turn and head God's way. *You must*, in fact! Feelings can often be the greatest enemy of truth. So even if in your heart of hearts you may not want to yield, be willing to go with God anyway, to surrender to this divine intervention that's shown up in the form of a mind-blowing interruption. You may still have an attraction to the things God has told you to leave behind, but your repentance is not negated just because your feelings haven't yet caught up with your resolve and determination. In the end repentance typically requires full dependence on the Spirit's power to help you stand against your inner desires and impulses.

Move on. Make a change. Then prayerfully depend on God to cause your feelings to follow.

My siblings and I recently bought our grandparents a new microwave. They desperately needed one. My spunky grandmother had braved her 1980s-era toaster oven much longer than she should have, and she wore the scars to prove it! She'd burned herself numerous times on some of the exposed, hot surfaces. Plus, the older this oven got, it took longer and longer for her food to cook. The thing had really become dangerous and inefficient for her to operate.

She grinned a huge smile when we walked into her house with that new machine, so grateful and appreciative. She watched intently as Jerry unplugged the old one from the wall and set the new one in its place.

But even though she was pleased to have the replacement unit, she balked a little when we told her we'd be hauling off her big, heavy original and taking it down to the dump to dispose of. Whether from the familiarity and attachment she felt with it after using it to prepare so many meals for herself and her husband through the years or from the practical side of her nature that hated to see something thrown away if it still basically seemed to work for her, she much preferred that we put it down in the basement—you know, "just in case."

Just in case? Just in case, what? She now had a shiny, new microwave right out of the box, plugged up and ready for years of use in her kitchen. She had no need for a backup, no reason for trying to cook with that sorry old scorcher ever again. This new appliance promised to make her life more satisfying, promised to keep her from being harmed or shocked by it when she least expected, promised to eliminate the time wasted from dealing with all those problems and slowdowns she'd been experiencing on a routine basis.

Yet, you know, she still kinda hated to lose the old one.

And in one way it's understandable. She'd been turning those dials for so long, they were probably indented with the ridges of her fingerprints. She could operate that unit in the dark if she had to. It had sat on that same countertop for so many years, it would feel weird for a while not seeing it there when she shuffled into the kitchen for her morning cup of coffee.

That old stuff can be comfortable to us. And comforting. The plan we'd arranged, the life ambitions we'd set in place, the image of this season of our lives we'd counted on—they're hard to let go of when He's asking us to yield to something new and unknown. We sort of miss having them around the house. We pine for them on days when we can't figure out how to defrost a pound of hamburger without reading the owner's manual.

We grow so accustomed to doing things the old way.

But God, through the merciful privilege of repentance, will give us some new things to do. He'll show us some more receptive, more obedient, even more exciting, expectant ways to respond to our divine interventions. And if we'll keep after them over time, we'll see these new changes and choices yielding enough fruit to counteract our initial feelings of avoidance. Like my grandmother, we may still have an affinity for the old things, our old attitudes, our old tastes and preferences, but when we act in conjunction with God's new direction, we ultimately discover the benefits of making the change.

So, out with the old! It's OK. What God has in store is so much better anyway.

—— Anything You Say ——

I want to be quick to point out, before any of us gets the wrong idea, that just because repentance takes a boatload of courage and commitment fueled by the Spirit's power doesn't mean it's nothing but simple brute force without any sensitivity or discernment. Repentance does not mean going in any good direction we choose but in going *God's* direction. And there can be a big difference.

The devil, you know, is never far away when repentance is going on or being contemplated. And if he fails at luring us back into our comfortable patterns, he'll likely try tempting us to choose a more comfortable method of making amends—something that *feels* like repentance to us even if it's not exactly what God is asking us to deal with.

Look carefully, for example, at Jonah's words:

> I will sacrifice to You with the voice of thanksgiving.
> That which I have vowed I will pay. (Jon. 2:9)

He was likely speaking of the thanksgiving or peace offerings prescribed in Leviticus 7, which included both animal sacrifice and cereal offering. And he promised to perform them "with the voice of thanksgiving." The sense of it "appears to be songs accompanying the making of a sacrifice."[12] Jonah not only intended to give actual sacrifices but also verbal ones—the "sacrifice of praise" (Heb. 13:15).

Nothing wrong, of course, with Jonah's desiring to return to Jerusalem and engage in completing his ceremonial rituals to the Lord. After what Jonah had done, you've got to be encouraged that he would seek to reengage with God in worship at all.

But to be quite frank about it, as admirable as this plan was, that's not what God had commanded Jonah to do. He had told him to go to Nineveh. Jerusalem was really in *Jonah's* direction, not God's. And while returning to the temple and his familiar religious surroundings was fine and good, it was never going to substitute for his disobedience in not fulfilling the calling of God on his life. That's why God's first words to Jonah after he was deposited back onto dry land mirrored those He'd spoken to him at the very beginning: "Arise, go to Nineveh" (3:2). All the unleavened cakes and wafers in the world, glazed with dutiful brushes of olive oil, presented to the Lord in solemn, grateful praise and honor, could not do for Jonah what only his willing, surrendered obedience could accomplish.

Making good by going to Nineveh was more important than making amends by going to Jerusalem.

Sometimes when we're caught red-handed in our rebellious running and we react to the pain by making our promises to change, we decide to go back to our Monday night Bible study. We pray more. We fast through the day on Fridays. We don't begin eating a meal, even in public, without saying a blessing. We do the things that make us feel spiritual, renewed, connected with God again.

Good.

But God is still seeking *relationship* with us and *obedience* from us, not just a religious reaction. He would prefer that we get *right* with Him rather than just behave for Him. And if we don't realize that, then the same evasions and avoidances we'd been displaying before—the ones God has been working to reveal to us by interrupting us, by intervening in our lives—may still persist even after we've said we're sorry and tried to patch things up with Him.

"To obey is better than sacrifice," the prophet Samuel had said to a misguided King Saul (1 Sam. 15:22), who thought his disobedience to a clear command from God could be overlooked by engaging in a religious exercise that showed what a big, spiritual guy he was. But although Yahweh had *allowed* sacrifices as a means of atoning for sin, they were not his ultimate desire. He longed for people who had a heart to obey Him and remain in fellowship with Him, not people who chose their own path and then ran to the altar to gain forgiveness for their actions. Offering a sacrifice was an easier option for Saul than his willing obedience.

We, too, have been known to disguise a measure of disobedience behind our "sacrifices"—well-meaning and heartfelt though they may be—thinking they cover and excuse us from having to deal any more deeply or personally with God. If we're faithful in church and singing in the choir and going on short-term mission trips, would He still expect us to deal with His latest command, to yield to His last set of instructions? Maybe, just maybe, we think we can do enough religious stuff to satisfy Him so He'll leave us alone. Hopefully, then, we won't have to say "yes" to any prompting of God that's always gotten a solid "no" from us before. Won't have to worry about responding to interruptions any differently than we ever do, not stopping to consider that they might be divine interventions—an invitation to participate with God in something eternally significant and supernatural.

But what was His word to you? What has God called you specifically to do? Are you doing it? Are you changing? Are you yielding to the divine intervention?

Our answers reveal if we are truly repentant.

— Jonah at the Crossroad —

This moment in Jonah's life—chapter 2, verse 9—is what many commentators believe to be the central message of his entire adventure, the hinge upon which the whole story hangs. "Salvation is from the LORD," Jonah declared. Not just to the Jews but to everyone. This is what God was challenging him not only to see and accept but to act on. To participate in. He was being told to move in conjunction with God's direction. To change. In fact, all of Israel was.

When the book of Jonah was written, its original purpose was to be read to the Israelites. God desired that Jonah's mission remind His chosen nation of something that would not have made sense to them—that God had a heart for others outside of Israel and wanted to dispense mercy to them as well. Even as late as the apostle Paul's day, this was considered a great "mystery"—the fact that Gentiles could somehow become "fellow heirs and fellow members of the body, and fellow partakers of the promise" (Eph. 3:6).

Incredible. Just couldn't be.

What a pity if Jonah had chosen to pass up this incredible opportunity to get on board with God's unbelievably stunning plans for humanity. What a pity if Israel did. More importantly, what a pity whenever we do. What mind-blowing experiences might we miss out on when we opt for old ways of doing things, our old plans and ambitions, our own path (which doesn't hold a candle to what He has in store), rather than looking past the known and familiar, expecting that God must be up to something special.

Really special.

Because when we drill down to the original language of Jonah 2:9, we see that the Hebrew word for "salvation" is a derivative of the name *Yeshua*—the same name that Mary would be told centuries later to give to her coming Son. "The Christian reader who hears this conclusion to Jonah's prayer in its original language cannot miss this word that sounds so much like the Hebrew name of Jesus, which has meant deliverance and salvation for the peoples of the world."[13] When God invites us to act in conjunction with His direction, He's not asking us to go without. He's intervening in order to involve us in something more thrilling and precious than we ever find in keeping to ourselves or staying within our cozy comfort zones. He is offering *Himself* to us—life with God—the most electrifying experience known to mortal man.

And if that doesn't change everything, I don't know what does.

So this key moment in Jonah's experience is a key moment for us to do business with God as well, to see if we're truly being reached by the reasons behind our interrupted life—our *divinely intervened* life.

- Is there anything (a mind-set, a relationship, an ambition, a lifestyle) we wouldn't relinquish if He asked us to?
- Are our hearts available at His command?
- Will we follow Him only so far and no farther?
- Is there an unspoken level of discomfort we will not tolerate when surrendering to Him?
- Could He ask something of us that we would simply not do?

This might be a good time to put down the book and deal squarely with these questions. It's not enough for us just to read them. We must recognize what they're asking. They may only require "yes" or "no" answers, but they go much deeper than that. They require us to say yes not only with our hearts but also our feet and our time and our calendars and our checkbooks— humbly obeying and responding to God's sovereign authority at any expense.

— Letting Go —

Jude has an affinity for acorns. I don't know what it is about those little brown nuts that pique his two-year-old interest so much, but whenever we go outside, he immediately begins scanning the horizon for them. He's become a little hoarder, trying to collect as many of them as he can in his grubby little hands. I watch and laugh as he insecurely juggles them all.

Last fall, before the weather turned unusually cold and snowy here in Dallas, I was outside with the boys almost every afternoon. One day Jude was scavenging on his normal acorn hunt when he came across a jar that one of his brothers had left outside the day before. All the critters they'd captured and confined inside had taken the opportunity of nightfall to escape, and yet a solitary acorn remained.

One lone acorn. Just sitting there in the jar. He *had* to have it!

Immediately he transformed into a miniature version of Sherlock Holmes, closely investigating the best way to get his trophy out. Finally he settled on a plan—working his hand into the narrow opening of the jar, fixing a firm grasp on the acorn, and with his hold firmly in place, removing it in his fist. But this last step proved a bit of a problem. His rounded fist with the acorn inside was too big to fit through and take out.

Hmm.

I watched him struggle for a while. Then when I could see the frustration setting in, I went over to help. (Must've not needed to brush my teeth this time!) His face was getting red. His voice was starting to raise. I tried explaining to him that if he'd just let go, I could pour the acorn out of the jar—easy as anything—and give it back to him in a way he could enjoy. But he would hear none of it. He just wasn't letting go.

For the next little while I watched my son walk around the yard with a glass jar dangling at the end of one arm—his fist still curled inside, his acorn still squeezed securely in his palm. But there wasn't much else he could do in the way of playtime as long as he continued holding on to that nut he wanted so badly. Everything was hindered and his enjoyment hampered, simply because . . . he wouldn't let go.

"Those who cling to worthless idols," the prophet Jonah declared from inside the fish, "forfeit the grace that could be theirs" (Jon. 2:8 NIV). When we stop the cycle of repentance from making that final, decisive turnaround onto the road back home, we give up the full, ongoing experience of God's faithful love. By hanging onto familiar sins, goals, ambitions, and other comforts that are unconducive with going God's direction, we lose so much more than we realize—more than any of those pursuits can ever hope to provide.

Whatever divine intervention the Lord has brought your way, has it revealed some things you're holding onto much too tightly? Has it hurt to experience the force of God's intervention, prying your fingers away, not to steal from you but to put something priceless and new in its place?

Jonah's knuckles must have been white with pain as God's holy hand forced his own hand open. Yet with palms flattened and empty, he raised his arms to the Lord in sweet surrender and vowed to go with God, even if it meant going to Nineveh.

It's your turn to do the same.

The change will look good on you.

Part 4

Second Chances

CHAPTER 10

There's More Where These Came From

Now the word of the LORD came to Jonah the second time, saying . . .

JONAH 3:1

I remember well the day I was sitting by the window in our bedroom, so struck by a single verse from the book of Jonah, I found myself sliding to my knees on the floor. I had earlier locked the door to ensure myself some peace and quiet with the Lord— (I have three little boys, remember?)—and now the Holy Spirit had *unlocked* His Word with one offhand statement so full of hope and promise, I could hardly contain the praise. With my hands extended upward toward the heavens, I voiced a prayer more full of spontaneous thanks than maybe any prayer I've uttered in a long time. God was speaking, and it was powerful.

I was enthralled.

In the first place, studying the prophet's abrupt calling from God somehow mirrored the shock I had felt upon learning that our two-parent, two-kid household was about to expand by one. My third pregnancy had caught me completely off guard. Totally unexpected. My life had again become a "life interrupted," only in a more substantial way than ever before. And something about Jonah's familiar Old Testament story seemed to hold examples and answers God wanted me to apply here, in my situation.

But if I needed any more confirmation from His Spirit that this particular Bible book had something significant to say to me, it was this one special moment alone at home, set against a pivotal moment from Scripture when "the word of the LORD came to Jonah the second time" (Jon. 3:1).

Don't let the simplicity or brevity of this line disguise its depth and power.

God spoke . . . for a second time.

He specializes in second chances.

When we've messed up. When we've rebelled. When we've recoiled at the plans He's unfolded before us, we still get another chance.

And don't we all just need to know that sometimes?

I know I sure did. And still do.

- Because I am Paul—the chief of sinners.
- I am Peter—the one who's made multiple promises to God that I couldn't (or wouldn't) keep.
- I am Samuel—the person who has often required God to call out to me time and time again before I finally realized He was speaking.
- And I am Jonah—one who, even when hearing a word from God clearly, has been known to turn and run in the opposite direction.

I've been known to see Him lining up circumstances in my life, leading me in a different way than I wanted or expected, perhaps speeding up or slowing down the timetable I'd fixed in my mind, and I have sometimes rebelled against His intervention.

I've seen it as nothing other than a rude, unwelcome interruption—the upset music career, the college romance lost, the television career derailed. I've often jumped to the wrong conclusions. And now, in my heart, I hadn't fully surrendered to the idea of our new baby and the changes required in this new phase of ministry God was calling us to. I wasn't doing a good job of yielding to His lordship and sovereignty. And I was ashamed of myself.

Yet God has given me a second chance. Again and again.

And for the life of me, I don't know why.

That sunny day in our bedroom, the full force of this grace-filled reality caught me at a place deep within my spirit. And I remember crying out to Him in grateful awe, "Lord, thank You for choosing to speak to me a second time, for not sitting up there distant and aloof on high with plans to put me on the shelf after I've turned my back on You, after I've failed to go along with what You were working to accomplish in me." Instead, He is still willing to speak to you and me today, still willing to use us, still looking forward to what He's going to help us do with a second opportunity.

I want to be the kind of follower who never gets over the blessing of being given another chance. I want to come to the place (after God's many faithful interventions) where I can say, "Lord, from this moment on, I'm willing to surrender to whatever You want me to do." I have made—and will still make—some bobbles and missteps in the execution, but I know He will keep offering me new possibilities to follow through. And while I never want to abuse this, I know how much I depend on His second chances.

It's worth praising Him for every day—this Father who has a tender heart toward His children, who derives real enjoyment out of forgiving, who loves us enough to let us try it again.

The word of the Lord did not just come. It came "a second time."

And that comes as thrilling news to me.

I know we've just traveled through a deep, underwater phase with Jonah where we've experienced again what it's like to be caught red-handed with exposed rebellion, with resistant hearts, with mind-sets unwilling to believe or even consider that God's slightly new plan for our lives is more fruitful than the one we'd already put on our agenda. If you're anything like me, you've seen some things about yourself during this stretch of our journey together that have not been easy to look at. You've not wanted to think you were capable of such how-dare-yous and back talk. You'd not actually recognized how inflexible and unmanageable you'd become toward God, how quickly your hands shoot up in protest when He starts taking you to places you don't want to go.

And like Jonah, as your heart has been illuminated by the highly effective searchlight of divine circumstances and consequences, perhaps you've felt a wave of guilt and condemnation that made you dead sure God wanted you "expelled" from His sight (Jon. 2:4).

But that's not the God you serve. That's not the God who keeps reaching out even when you've been pulling back. "Look again" toward His "holy temple," as Jonah did (v. 4). Stand and receive a grace you can never outrun, a divine mercy whose reach defies all boundaries.

Welcome your second chance, even in the midst of an unwelcome interruption.

It's another gift from your heavenly Father.

My husband, Jerry, is never more attractive to me than when he's caught one or more of our boys in some obvious fault but then decides to give the guys a second chance. I'll see them looking up at their big ol' daddy, nervously concerned about the discipline they know they deserve. But then—without excusing or overlooking what they've done—I've seen him bend down, kiss them on the cheek, and send them on their way to live another day. That really does it for Mama.

Just like God has done it for me. And for you.

"The word of the LORD came to Jonah the second time." This snapshot from the life of a resistant prophet is in many ways the pinnacle of his entire story. And I'm hoping and praying it's the word from God you've been needing to hear today—perhaps needing to hear for a long time. Thank the Lord for second, third, fourth, fifth, fiftieth, and five hundredth chances. No amount of running and hiding exempts us from being sought and found and patterned back into His plan for our lives.

Just call Him the "hound of heaven."

—— Dance of the Redeemed ——

This second-chance theme is hardly the exclusive property of Jonah's biblical real estate. God's blueprint for manufacturing new opportunities is seen in His people's lives from one end of Scripture to the other.

The brothers of Joseph, for example, appear in the book of Genesis as a jealous, conniving brood, out to wreak resentful vengeance on their somewhat boastful yet mostly just boldly honest kid brother. A father's favoritism had tossed fuel on the fire, making them feel more than justified in fighting back against the betrayal. So in a heartless act of hatred and abandon, they sold Joseph as a slave bound for Egypt, hoping never to see him again. But when famine brought them out of the Hebrew woodwork and into Egypt to seek help and supplies, their divine appointment with Joseph brought their rash deeds home to roost. They fully expected to pay for their prior offenses with the currency of their own lives. But Joseph, wielding the power and authority to return the cruel favor, presented them instead with the gift of a second chance, knowing that God had meant "for good" what they had pursued in evil (Gen. 50:20).

Second chances.

Aaron probably always felt like a second fiddle to his younger brother Moses. Yet the role God was preparing to give him as high priest, officiating in the tabernacle, was highly significant in its own right. He would enjoy the privilege of entering the most holy place, experiencing the delight of God's presence in ways that few others ever would. But while Moses was up on Mount Sinai, receiving (among other things) instructions for the making of Aaron's priestly garments and his consecration practices, Aaron was downhill acting in a most unholy fashion, caving to the people's frenzied desire for a substitute god. Yet even after Aaron had failed so profoundly as a leader, God didn't jump to find a replacement and reassign him to the scrap heap. He gave him a second chance, still appointing him to serve as high priest, even after his public demonstration of poor judgment (see Exod. 29–32).

Second chances.

Only once in Jesus' teaching did He present three parables in a row to communicate a single point. But when He did, He used the opportunity to convey the restorative nature of the Father's heart (see Luke 15). He chose a lost sheep, a lost coin, and a lost son as unforgettable analogies about the way God handles His possessions, whether misplaced by our foolishness or our carelessness.

The message of these parables would have been revolutionary to the first-century Jewish mind. Rarely if ever had they considered a God who would seek out and search for the lost, like a shepherd noticing that one of his precious flock had slipped away and steered off the beaten path. They didn't tend to think He cared that much or would expend so much energy on one lost soul. Yet the clear conclusion is that the heart of our servant Savior seeks out, saves, and salvages those He loves, people like us who don't even know how much danger we're in, who've chosen to turn our backs on Him deliberately or just slowly wander away by degrees from His best plans for us.

Second chances.

They're what our God is all about.

And when we get them—like the shepherd locating his lost sheep, the woman recovering her lost coin, the father receiving his prodigal son back from the wild—we should rejoice like there's no tomorrow, the way these three did. There shouldn't be enough words to adequately describe our praise.

A young man at my church named Daniel has become recognizable in the midst of our fellowship. He sits on the front row every Sunday. And each week without fail, in the large carpeted area between the platform and the first row of seats, Daniel dances before the Lord.

You should know that I don't go to a dancing kind of church. I mean, we raise our hands, we speak out loud a little, and we don't mind getting really happy about Jesus while we're at it, but we don't do much if any dancing in the aisles. None of this matters to Daniel, however, who takes his chosen place every Sunday without fail and enters into worship by doing what Daniel does. He dances. And frankly, I've often wondered where this ongoing urge of his comes from.

Well, recently I asked him. And found out.

Daniel was born to a mentally ill mother and was then adopted by his grandparents. But they lived in a tough, underprivileged area of town where trouble usually came looking for young kids, even if they weren't exactly looking for *it*. When his godly grandfather died, Daniel lost about the only thing that had been keeping him from falling even deeper into the drug culture that consumed his school and neighborhood. And one fateful day, in the midst of a drug deal gone horribly wrong, Daniel pulled the trigger on a gun that killed a person in cold blood. As a result, he was sentenced to spend every moment until his eighteenth birthday in the custody of the Texas Youth Commission, with his adult sentencing to follow at that time.

How he dreaded turning eighteen—with a much greater intensity than most people look forward to it—because while the youth correctional center was certainly no picnic, it was nothing like doing hard time in the state pen. Every day that inched closer to that monumental teenage milestone, his stomach turned one twist tighter. His dread of the future grew meaner and nastier, more frightening to think about.

Little did he know, when he walked into that wood-paneled courtroom on his eighteenth birthday, that the change in his life was about to be for the better. *Way* better. The grandmother of his shooting victim had composed a handwritten letter to the authorities, asking the courts to "please give this young man a second chance." And the judge, moved by the compassion of a grieving grandma, gave a recommendation for leniency in Daniel's case. His sentence was suspended. He was free to walk out the door with nothing more than a parole period to serve.

"And I will dance in front of this church until the day I die," he told me, "because when you've been given a second chance, you've got something to dance about."

And if a man vomited out of a fish after three days in its digestive tract has any strength left in his legs at all, I'm guessing Jonah did a bit of a jig along that sandy stretch of oceanfront when he got his.

Second chances call for a celebration.

—— Chance of a Lifetime ——

Yom Kippur, the Day of Atonement, is considered by many practicing Jews as the highest holy day on the religious calendar. It's the most solemn fast of the Jewish year, the last of the ten days of penitence, commemorating (interestingly enough, since we've sort of touched on it in this chapter) the giving of a second set of tablets to Moses after he shattered the first ones in rage upon seeing Aaron's golden calf spectacle occurring in the foothills of Sinai. But even more interesting to us, in light of this book, is that the centerpiece of the Yom Kippur afternoon service—known as the *Mincha*—involves a public reading of the entire book of Jonah. If God could forgive Nineveh, the thinking goes, and if God could forgive Jonah, He can surely forgive us. If repentance means anything, if there's any hope to be found after our failure to respond to God in complete surrender and yieldedness, Jonah is exhibit A. This short, four-chapter sliver of his life we get to read about and study is a working theology of God's compassionate offer of second chances.

And so are we.

Now I don't want to leave you with the impression that second chances suddenly transform our lives from being impossibly tough to blissfully simple, from being hard as a rock to being easy as pie. (We'll look at this more fully in the next chapter.) They're not merely a sweet sigh of relief and a new spring in your step. But for now I just want you to know that getting back on your feet and being able to continue living is always a possibility for the child of God. If you've been doubting this lately, if you think God has moved on to somebody else who shows greater promise and more faithful patience than you do, you're not reading Him right. And you're not reading Jonah.

"The word of the LORD came to Jonah the second time" (Jon. 3:1). That means you too. No matter what you've done. No matter what you *haven't* done. No matter what attitude you've copped or what pity party you've thrown. No matter how often your life has shown a lot of Jonah's qualities in it, perhaps even as recently as this week.

Second chances are a sign of God's deep, abiding love for you.

One of the most remarkable documentaries I've ever seen is titled *A Man Named Pearl*, the true account of a blue-collar African-American who wasn't wanted in his rural South Carolina neighborhood because they feared he wouldn't keep up his yard, that his mere presence would drag down the property values of those living around him.

But he was intent on proving them wrong. After working twelve hours a day at his regular job, Pearl Fryar would come home, take his lawn equipment out of the shed, and spend the rest of the evening—sometimes into the wee hours of the morning—tending to the weeds and needs of his three-and-a-half acres of green space. Not only was he mowing and trimming around the edges, but he was also crafting enormous topiaries, transforming a patch of rough ground into a lush, manicured, truly incredible sight to behold.

Today horticultural students from area universities come there to learn from the creations he's made. Art teachers wander through to study his techniques and capture his imagination. Tourists drive in from miles around, mesmerized by the beauty and serenity of the place.

He's done more than win the "yard of the month" designation a time or two. He's put little Bishopville, South Carolina—population 3,670, when everybody's home—on the map.

But what really fascinates me about Pearl Fryar's story is that when he first started work on what would become his award-winning garden, he walked into one of the local nurseries and told the manager that he'd noticed some little seedlings and plants sitting out on their back dock, like they were just going to be thrown away. If so, he wondered if anyone would mind if he took some of them. Getting a favorable reply, he pulled his truck behind the building, loaded up the fledgling plants that had been discarded from the store's sellable stock, drove them to his house, and today they form the backbone of his gardening masterpiece.

Second chances. None of us deserves them, yet the Master Gardener comes to where we are, picks us up in our useless, discarded, discouraged condition, and replants us in the places where He knows we're most likely to grow.

One of the key places (if not *the* place) where I feel the most humbled at the gracious, miraculous, "Pearl Fryar-like" work God has done in my life is when I'm on a platform teaching. With my Bible perched under one arm, my notes tucked inside, my heart palpitating, my eyes scanning the crowd, I ask the audience to bow their heads for a quick prayer before I continue. I'm praying not only because I need God's empowerment but because I need a minute to gain my composure. You see, I'm stunned. Every single time I get ready to open God's Word and teach from it, I'm in complete disbelief. I have no business being here. There is no reason under the sun why God would give me the opportunity to open His Word and declare it to His people. Because I've been Jonah. I've so often chosen a lifestyle out of sync with His purposes. I've so often missed His signals because I was too wound up in reading my own. I've so often failed to follow because I wasn't sure I could trust Him and was a lot more interested in feeling under control than living under His authority.

Yet for some reason He lets me partner with Him. For some reason He gives me beauty for ashes. There's no other explanation for it than His grace. And there's no other suitable response than a shout of grateful praise.

God hasn't given up on us, my friend. Aren't you glad?

Thank the Lord, for a second chance.

CHAPTER 11

Rinse and Repeat

"Arise, go to Nineveh the great city and proclaim to it the proclamation which I am going to tell you."

JONAH 3:2

I'll admit, I was a little slow hopping on board, and I'm still not the most technologically savvy person in the world—(only one per household, please, and my husband definitely has the corner on that)—but let me just say in my own defense, I've gotten pretty adept at this texting business. Give me a few seconds and the tip of my right thumb, and you'd almost swear I was fifteen. I can flat get with it! Even on my Twitter account, with only 140 characters available per message, I've become masterful at saying a lot with a little. Shortcuts have become my standard operating procedure.

One little thing I've noticed, however. My texting chops may be high adolescent caliber. Nimble and refined. But because my "homework" often consists of writing books and Bible studies, as opposed to science and geometry quizzes, people expect me to communicate in full sentences. And my busy-mom-with-three-kids brain sometimes forgets to flip the switch from cell phone to laptop. So even when I'm working on serious stuff, with various Bible translations and commentaries and study books circled about me, my typing fingers can sometimes go all OMG and LOL (translation: "oh, my goodness" and "laugh out loud") and B4 I know it, I've been up 2 this 4 hours. Can U believe that?

Yeah, shortcuts are great for texting and tweeting. Or when you're short a half stick of butter for a cookie recipe. Or when you're needing to cut ten minutes off a traffic tie-up. But shortcuts are not always the best choice to make. In fact, I think I can say without any fear of overstating: there are *no* shortcuts with God. Even on second chances.

Jonah, for example, had been severely disciplined for his resistance to God's original calling and plan. He had the wet clothes, the pruny fingers, and that unmistakable fishy smell about him to prove it. But when his second chance came via some pretty major projectile vomiting on the big fish's part, the Scripture doesn't say but "it is reasonable to assume Jonah was right back near Joppa where he started."[14]

Imagine how stunned he must have been—first to realize he was still alive; next to recognize the familiar seashore of Joppa; and then to hear the same divine instructions he'd been given before— "Arise, go to Nineveh the great city" (Jon. 3:2). There would be no getting out of God's will for him, no shortcut to this Assyrian stronghold. Full, detailed obedience would still be required.

See, Jonah's second chance wasn't a detour back to Jerusalem and away from responsibility, even though going there to make his sacrifices seemed like a noble, reasonable thing to do. Neither was his second chance a free ticket to the front gates of Nineveh. Five hundred miles still stood between his current location and his mission field. And so the hard work of obedience—the one-foot-in-front-of-the-other variety—was every bit as real and expected of him at this second-chance moment as it had been at the beginning. Jonah, having been through the wringer, was much more committed now to going through with this—something he hadn't been before—but I wonder if he at least wished for an easier way to get it done.

Like Abraham. He'd been willing at first to believe God's audacious promises of a family tree that produced more descendants than stars in the sky or sands on the seashore. But with no children of his own to start the ball rolling and none apparently on the horizon, he decided a shortcut was his best option—an illicit relationship that yielded a son, as well as the added benefit of not having to wait on God's timetable. As if that was going to work (see Gen. 16:1–4).

Like the rich young man who came to Jesus, hoping to punch his ticket to paradise with a dog-and-pony show promoting his impressive line of good deeds—a well-worn shortcut that seemed a lot more convenient and efficient than parting with his pride, his independence, and most importantly (to him) his money (see Luke 18:18–25).

Even Satan himself knows the unbelievably tragic effects of taking shortcuts, or else he wouldn't have offered them so desperately and deceptively to Jesus in the wilderness, tempting Him with easier, quicker, less painful ways of accomplishing His mission—performing miracles just to satisfy His hunger, putting on a public show to attract attention, making deals with the devil to secure His hold on power and authority. None of these fazed Jesus, however. He understood there was no shortcut to following through on what His Father had given Him to do (see Matt. 4:1–11).

And it's the same with us. God has intervened with a challenge—perhaps a huge one. Like the woman I met recently whose daughter had been involved in a tragic situation of some kind, leaving this ready-to-rest grandmother the task of becoming a full-time parent all over again . . . of her grandbabies. Any of the shortcuts around this enormous interruption would've resulted in much less wear and tear on a grandmother's body, a grandmother's endurance, a grandmother's ability to bounce back from a full day of babysitting. But she is clear on what God is asking her to do. And to be obedient to what He has set before her, only the direct route would do. Hers won't be just grandma's house. It will be home.

No shortcuts.

—— Last Things First ——

Jonah's miraculous rescue at sea had changed a lot about his circumstances. He'd gotten a real taste of what running from God can do to a person. He'd found himself restored to a state of being he'd abandoned all hope of ever experiencing again: alive and breathing and standing on dry land. But even with this remarkable turn of events—this divinely conceived second chance—the core of God's instructions to the prophet remained unchanged: "Arise, go to Nineveh the great city." God told him to do exactly the same thing in chapter 3 that Jonah had tried to skirt around in chapter 1.

Jonah was back to square one.

And obedience was still *job* one.

No shortcuts.

He was not excusing him or letting him off the hook just because he'd been through a long, hard, tiring ordeal. We must be careful not to misinterpret a second chance as meaning that God has kind of forgotten about what happened when we had our *first* chance. He hasn't just agreed to disagree with us about this.

So as you move forward and consider what God might have you to do next, I suggest you think back to the last thing He asked you to do—the original instruction you backed out on or threw a fit about, the thing you decided wasn't really in keeping with what a person in your position should have to endure . . . and start there.

Was it an apology you needed to make to your spouse—but didn't? Or maybe an opportunity to end all this fighting and arguing with each other by simply relinquishing your right to win a point—but you wouldn't?

Was it a financial gift you felt stirred to contribute to some missionaries who were passing through at church, but the twenty-five dollars in your pocket was supposed to buy your lunch on the way home, so you kept it?

Was it an act of service for a friend or family member you should have performed without employing the martyr complex, making sure they knew what it cost you and how much you'd been put upon?

Was it an urging to get involved in ministry that, as you often do, you just ascribed to your codependent conscience and took the easy way out, avoiding it altogether?

Was it yielding to a major life change, like a special-needs child or a cross-country move you were sour about embarking on?

God intervened in your life. And you didn't like it. You had other things to do. You had other stuff on your mind. You had several points of objection to what He was suggesting and implying. And so you chose to handle it your own way rather than His.

You ran. You refused. You tried to go around it or just flat get out of it.

And you may have even done it in a way you hoped others wouldn't know about and judge you for. Consider Jonah, for example, who with this second chance "arose and went" (3:3) to Nineveh. It's interesting that this is the same action he took in the first chapter: "Jonah rose . . . [and] went" (v. 3). Without close examination it could have appeared to many that he was being obedient with all this "arising and going" and everything. But no matter how similar the two actions appeared, only one represented Jonah's being obedient to the calling of God on his life.

Sure, we can impersonate obedience when we don't want to follow along with what God is demanding of us—not only what He's asking of our physical presence but also of our heart, our will, our focus, our attention? Internal running helps us get away with it in others' eyes, but you know if you've been upfront and fully compliant in your obedience and surrender to God.

Second chances, then, are no time to put on airs or to put up a front. This is no time to drag out the same old excuses we've used before, or to consider that little matter from last week, last month, or last year suddenly overlooked and escaped. No, this is your new opportunity to do what you didn't do the first go-around—fully, completely, and authentically.

So head back to Joppa, recall the last set of instructions He gave you, and get busy being obedient about that.

That's what Jonah had to do.

That's what second chances are for.

—— More than Meets the Eye ——

Jonah was a man who'd made his prophetic livelihood by being precise about what God was saying to him. So I'm guessing he probably noticed the slight difference in the Lord's renewed command to him the second time. Yes, it was similar. At first it may have felt like *déjà vu*. Yet there was a bit more on the table than had been there before.

Arise, go to Nineveh the great city and cry against it, for
their wickedness has come up before Me. (Jon. 1:2)

That was the initial command. Now this:

Arise, go to Nineveh the great city and proclaim to it the
proclamation which I am going to tell you. (Jon. 3:2)

Much the same, only different.

Nineveh remained as the destination for Jonah's mission, but
God's directives had slightly changed. In chapter 1, the instructions were far more implicit. God told Jonah exactly what to do
when he got there. This second time, however, included one additional tier of responsibility. Jonah still knew that his obedience
required a one-way ticket out of town. He was still aware that
he must make a bold pronouncement to the Ninevites. But now,
instead of simply being required to pack up and go, he must keep
his ears open later for further instructions about what his message was going to be—"the proclamation which I am going to tell
you." No carry-on bag of prepackaged plans and details.

And definitely no shortcuts.

In one way God only seemed to be making things harder on
him. Upping the ante. Perhaps it's somewhat like a parent not
only telling her child to take back the bubble gum he stole from
the store but also making him apologize in person to the manager. Now he'll also have the added responsibility of tidying up a
broken relationship. This way he'll have a harder time forgetting
that disobedience is never as much fun as it looks like, and that
front-end obedience is always worth what it costs.

However, what might have felt like added pressure and
demands to Jonah was actually just an added promise—that if
Jonah took care of the obedience part, if he didn't give in to
the temptation to hedge his bets or try meeting God halfway, the
Lord could be counted on to do Jonah's speaking for him and tell

him exactly what to say. Because if God was going to be feeding him the message, then God's presence had to be there to do it.

Yes, God's *presence* was going with him.

I don't know if that felt like good news to Jonah. And it may not always feel like the most comforting news to us either—not as comfortable sounding as maybe hanging back and not going at all. Not as convenient and cost-efficient as the shortcut we'd prefer to take. But if God has asked you to be obedient in a specific area that leaves you frightened, vulnerable, alone, or overwhelmed, guess what? He's promised to be right there with you.

And that's really all you need to know.

That's why shortcuts are as unnecessary as they are disobedient—because God has promised you His presence. He's going in there with you. You don't have to hold back part of your heart and emotions to keep from being hurt. You don't have to look around to see what others are doing. You don't have to check to see if your friends and family approve. You can go all in. You can just follow every nudge and piece of instruction He gives you. You can do a spiritual cannonball right into the deep end of life. No shortcuts necessary . . . because God's Spirit will be there every second to guide you along.

In the Old Testament the Holy Spirit was only given to certain believers at certain times to accomplish certain tasks. Then whenever that task was complete (or perhaps earlier, if the person sinned or rebelled), the Holy Spirit removed Himself from that individual. So I'd like to think the promise and awareness that God's presence would be an ongoing source of information, provision, and empowerment to Jonah, even in the midst of his lingering fears and conflicted emotions, would've been a profound encouragement to him. I hope so.

But I know for sure it can be an encouragement to us—those of us who are God's children by grace through faith, who stand on this side of Christ's atoning cross and empty tomb, who walk around each day with the blessed Holy Spirit guiding, directing, pointing things out, turning our focus, setting up encounters, putting thoughts in our heads and words in our mouths.

How easily we forget what a blessing and privilege this is, especially when we're running from an interruption.

Think of Jesus' disciples in John 16, tense amid the electric atmosphere leading up to what appeared to be an imminent death threat to their beloved Master. Alone with His closest followers on that scary, emotional night, Jesus confirmed to them that, yes, He would be leaving them. This was a drastic interruption if there had ever been one.

> But I tell you the truth, it is to your advantage that
> I go away; for if I do not go away, the Helper will not
> come to you; but if I go, I will send Him to you. (v. 7)

This Helper surely seemed to them like a poor substitute for having Jesus right there in the flesh. Rather than needing to exercise whatever spiritual muscles would be required to interact with this invisible Spirit, it was a whole lot easier just walking up to Jesus and asking Him whatever they were wondering about. They *loved* hanging out with Him. And the last thing they wanted was to see this interrupted.

But with Jesus preparing to leave them in the near future, they would need an internal compass to help them find their way. They had not been able to take enough notes over the course of their three years with Him to navigate every obstacle and interruption that lingered on the horizon. Couldn't have. But they *needn't* have because God's wise and wonderful Spirit would be there to guide them the rest of the way with step-by-step instructions, like a tour guide shepherding them from place to place, giving them the ideal amount of information they needed, precisely when they needed it. If they'd listen, He'd speak and direct them.

If they'd follow, He'd lead. And when it was all said and done, they'd be assured a life well lived and a journey well taken.

This presence of God that was promised to Jonah and to Jesus' disciples is the same Holy Spirit available to each of us as we walk in obedience to Him. When we're unclear on what to do, not knowing what to say, a bit fuzzy on how all of this fits together into some semblance of meaning and purpose, or tempted to take the shortcut route because we aren't sure we can handle what's being asked of us, we can trust with full assurance that He is here, doing His job, supplying just what we need exactly when we need it.

Friend, we've just got to learn to lay back in that. These arms are big and strong enough to hold us through anything! By offering us His eternal presence on an intimate, personal level, God is not making our lives more difficult. On the contrary He is giving us exactly what we need to keep from being mired down in guilt, agitation, and distance from Him. He is providing us full supply for every circumstance, even the hardest, most unexpected ones.

Is He sending you to Nineveh? Then His presence is going with you—meaning, you have no need for shortcuts, regardless of how daunting a task this is.

He knows, for example, you can't be the mama those kids really need in your own strength, with your own baggage, fulfilling all the other obligations that are on you. That's why God has given His Spirit to you—to help you be what you cannot.

He knows, single woman, you can't live a pure, holy, and righteous lifestyle in this sex-crazed world of ours, not without leaning on more support than whatever's built into your self-restraint and willpower. That's why God has given His Spirit to you—to help you stand up and be a light for Christ Jesus no matter what your other dating friends are doing.

He knows, sir, that you can't work enough hours, make enough time for your family, *and* fully devote yourself to church involvement. That's why God has given you His Spirit—to compensate for your limitations by multiplying every single effort you offer in His name, every time you trust His strength to be made visible through your weakness.

Jonah obviously didn't have the courage or desire to go to Nineveh on his own. That's why God gave him a new spin on his marching orders—to help him not only successfully participate in God's will but also to deepen His trust and confidence when facing the next interruption.

As sure as God gives us second chances, He gives us His Spirit to guide us, to counsel us, and to equip us for every turn along the journey.

You're not going to your Nineveh alone. So the lure to take shortcuts may be tempting, but it's completely unnecessary.

God's Spirit is going with you.

— Equal Opportunity —

Nineveh was no Mayberry. Even though it may not have been the hugest of places by today's population standards, it was thought to be home to nearly 600,000 inhabitants,[15] probably the "biggest, strongest, and wealthiest city of its day."[16] To citizens of the ancient Near East, it was absolutely enormous, "an exceedingly great city, a three days' walk" (Jon. 3:3).

In addition, most scholars believe that God hadn't merely called Jonah to proclaim His message to Nineveh proper but to all the surrounding towns and villages that depended on this major hub for protection and alliance. Plus, as mentioned earlier, Nineveh's formidable size was matched by an equally if not more daunting atmosphere of extreme evil, brutality, and violence.

Think big city. Think high crime. Think walking alone down a back street, feeling the eyes leer in your direction, looking for a safe place to stay the night, that petrified look on your face when you wonder if somebody's about to lunge out and come after you.

So with each sandy step Jonah took in that direction—five hundred miles of them—the impossibility of what God had called him to do must have pulsed through every extremity, making his desire for a shortcut more pressing than ever, leading him to conjure up all kinds of creative dodges and detours around this enormous assignment.

Maybe he should take the time to work up some good lines to say while he walked along—you know, in case he couldn't really depend on God to take care of that for him, or in case he might not like what God decided to tell him. Maybe he should take one more little side trip and rest up a bit more. That fish belly incident had really taken a lot out of him. Maybe he should go back and see if he could talk somebody into going with him for moral support.

But when a divine intervention is at work, an "exceedingly great" challenge translates into an "exceedingly great" opportunity. And the more daunting the task before you, the more fabulous the opportunity God is giving you to see His power at work.

I was seventeen when I visited Haiti on a mission trip, where I met a tiny young girl by the name of Manette. She was nine years old, living in what were undeniably the most deplorable conditions I had ever witnessed. It was one of those moments when you feel so full of compassion and desire to help yet so small and helpless. But outside of hugs and play and a little one-on-one attention for a short time frame, there seemed to be nothing I could do to make any real difference in that little girl's life or in the lives of those around her. The circumstances were just too dire.

Still, I couldn't get her out of my mind. Even back at home in my comfortable air-conditioned existence, I thought back to the heat and filth and want of that impoverished island nation and the look on Manette's face, a little girl who knew nothing else. She had captured my heart. God had interrupted my life with her need. And though insecure about how to communicate with her, doubting that such a small effort from one person like me could do any good, and tempted just to put the whole thing out of my mind, I decided to try. By God's grace and through the partnership of those who minister there in Haiti on a daily basis, I began sending letters and dollars and tightly compressed care packages to Manette, hoping she'd sense the love of an American friend and, more importantly, the love of Christ through me.

In January 2010, news broke that a devastating earthquake had rocked the island of Haiti. Thousands were dead. Whole villages and buildings demolished. Even the president had been forced to flee his palace and relocate to other quarters. And Manette, who had e-mailed me only a few days earlier, was likely in the hard-hit capital city of Port au Prince, having just entered her first year of nursing school.

It would be three long, anxious days before my phone calls and messages to the missions organization finally triggered a response. To my great relief I learned that Manette had made it through with only a few scratches—not only surviving but now busy helping in nearby Pignon where many had fled for safety. She was serving and sharing the love of Christ, a young woman transformed by our Savior's seeking heart.

I thought back to the day when I first met her, when the challenge of making a connection with a little girl so far away and so desperately in need seemed so terribly impossible. These many years later I've enjoyed a deep personal friendship for two decades with someone only God could've placed in my path. His intervention became an opportunity to love and be loved and be a small part of His plans for a young girl He had been drawing to Himself before the foundation of the world. She'd sensed God's love to her through others, and this compelled her to pass it on to those now in desperate need.

Sometimes His interventions feel like they're asking more than we can do. Costs too much. Hurts too much. Involves too much work, too many other people. Honestly there's probably a lot of truth to such concerns. But because God is calling, our job is not to obsess over the challenges but merely to trust what He's saying—not to focus on how little one person can do but embrace the opportunity of watching God do something incredible.

We get second chances. We get God's presence. And what's more, we get the "exceedingly great" opportunity of being part of something way bigger than we are, right in the middle of our ordinary lives.

Can't ask much more of an interruption than that.

—— What, How, Where ——

If you remember your Old Testament, you've likely heard of Naaman, the grizzled army captain who contracted leprosy and in his desperation sought help from an Israelite prophet, Elisha. But he sure didn't like Elisha's prescription for healing: "Go and wash in the Jordan seven times, and your flesh will be restored to you and you will be clean" (2 Kings 5:10).

Naaman wasn't happy with *what* he was being told to do, *how* he was being told to do it, or *where* he was being told to go. He'd been hoping for more of a bingo, bango, instant relief kind of healing. Just say the magic words and get this done with. And even if the whole dipping in the river thing was a necessary part of the plan, he thought a much cleaner, much more convenient alternative would be to use the water sources in his own hometown that were a lot nicer to swim in, plus a lot easier to get to.

Shortcuts. Bargains. Counterproposals.

Nice try, Naaman.

For what he obviously didn't understand when he "turned and went away in a rage" (v. 12) was that his cure wasn't in the water; it was in his obedience to the word of God. The work that God is trying to accomplish in and through us can only be found in our doing *what* He says, *how* He says to do it, and *where* He says to go. Full participation is the price of full reward.

As my friend Shundria often says to her three children, after giving them a task or chore to complete, "You can do it now, or you can do it later, but guess what: you're *gonna* do it." I think second-chance Jonah would concur with that.

So, yes, it's encouraging to see that "Jonah arose and went to Nineveh according to the word of the LORD" (Jon. 3:3). After all of that running and messing around, he'd been brought back to square one by the fatherly, sovereign, supervising hand of God— not to shame him but just to show him that shortcuts won't cut it. Not where following the Lord is concerned.

If you're sitting on a second chance, let it take you back to where you came from, where you last ran from an interruption, when you couldn't bring yourself to follow along with what God was sending you into. What you'll find on your return trip is a new, repentant heart, a greater sense of God's presence, and a fresh opportunity to obey—and then just see what happens next.

For Jonah, it was "rinse and repeat." Out of the fish and back into God's service.

What'll it be for you?

CHAPTER 12

Go to Nineveh

Go therefore and make disciples of all the nations, baptizing them in the name of the Father and the Son and the Holy Spirit.

MATTHEW 28:19

The name Brian "Head" Welch may not register in your memory banks, but if you know anything about heavy metal music (and I really, really *don't*), you're probably familiar with the band Korn and one of the founding members of their group—guitarist Head Welch.

First time I heard of him, I was flipping television channels in a Nashville hotel room, having arrived in town with my sister for a speaking event the following day. As I zoomed across the cable landscape, my remote finger happened to stop at a split-screen interview on CNN with a telltale hard rocker—the bare arms, the long hair, the black shirt, the eye mascara, the incredible collage of tattoos. And just before my short attention span prepared to gun the throttle toward another entertainment location, I heard the interviewer ask an interesting question: "So why did you stop playing in the band? What brought that decision about? What changed for you?"

What followed was one of the coolest, most captivating testimonies I'd ever heard in my life—*definitely* the best one I'd ever heard on a mainstream news outlet.

Brian Welch and Korn had become major players on the modern music scene. But in fairly typical fashion, his surge toward superstardom had dissolved into the familiar storylines of supermarket tabloids. Fame and fortune had led to international touring, available sex, crystal meth, and a slowly collapsing prison of pleasure-based despair. His wife had left, abandoning him with their only daughter. His drug addiction had escalated, spinning him further and further out of control. He was rolling in money, drunk on celebrity, . . . and slowly but surely dying inside.

Then unexpectedly, something new started happening.

A real estate broker (and Christian) who had been handling some of Brian's investments said to him one day, "Man, I've never done this before in my life, and I sure don't want to weird you out, but a Scripture verse came to me while I was reading my Bible today, and I felt like it was something I needed to share with you. Matthew 11:28: "Come to me, all you who are weary and burdened, and I will give you rest" (NIV).

Something clicked inside Brian when he heard it. Those life-rich words—weary, burdened, rest—set him to thinking. Two weeks later, still high on drugs, wearing a hooded shirt and thick with goth-style makeup, he stumbled into a church on Sunday morning and heard about a God who could make bad things fall off of you. He was drawn to that part. Seemed like just what he needed. So when the time came, he walked down the aisle and accepted Christ. Secretly he really hoped that having Jesus around would make him feel better about life without actually having to do the hard work of facing down an addiction or changing much.

Within a week, however, Jesus did the hard work for him. Sitting at home one morning, helplessly snorting another line of drugs but deep down wanting to be a better father, wanting to be a better man, Brian called out for help from above. "And I'm telling you, supernaturally, the taste for the drugs, the taste for the alcohol, they just left my mouth that very day. I felt a high that took me higher than any drug, any stage performance, anything I'd ever done in my life. I was instantly addicted to God right then and there."

"Are you saying this was like a deliverance?" the interviewer asked him.

"Yeah, that's exactly what I'm saying."

"And *who* did you say did this for you?" (Ooo, he walked right into that one, didn't he?)

"Jesus Christ, Son of the living God."

By this time my sister and I were doing a little happy dance on the hotel bed. The work and witness of the Lord Jesus were going forth from the studios of a secular news outfit and into the millions of homes that make up their viewing demographic. It was an awesome moment.

Several months later I got a call from the folks at the *Life Today* television program, asking if I'd be interested in appearing on one of their upcoming broadcasts. They were going to be taping four shows on this particular night coming up, and they were proposing that I be featured on two of them. When the filming date rolled around, I got there early to take advantage of the free meal they provide beforehand—(Mama didn't raise no fool)—and who do you think was sitting directly across from me at the dinner table but their other invited guest for the night: Brian "Head" Welch!

Every ounce of giddiness I had felt in that hotel room bubbled through me all over again, and I suddenly became—in a way I had never been before (or ever will again)—a heavy metal groupie. I told him how I'd seen him on television, how my sister and I had prayed for him, how impressed I was with his public boldness for Christ. And I can tell you from seeing and talking with him up-close, this is no lame stunt to hog the spotlight or to make a grandstand play. He's the real deal. As far as I'm concerned and from what little I know, Head Welch rocks!

He'd been given a second chance. And second chances can change everything. Especially when God reaches out to save a lost and dying soul.

The ultimate second chance.

My purpose in writing this book is primarily to help folks like you and me learn how to see our life interruptions as divine interventions and begin surrendering to the authority and sovereignty of the Lord Jesus Christ. I also want to remind us to receive and respond well to our second chances when we've blown the first ones.

But we would be dodging one of the main themes from the book of Jonah if we leave from here thinking that second chances are all about us.

God's command to Jonah—"Arise, go to Nineveh the great city and proclaim to it the proclamation which I am going to tell you" (Jon. 3:2)—might sound very "Old Testament," but it crosses a sturdy bridge into the New Testament principle of evangelism, as spoken in the words of Jesus to the disciples of His day and, by extension, to the church every day since:

> Go therefore and make disciples of all the nations,
> baptizing them in the name of the Father and
> the Son and the Holy Spirit. (Matt. 28:19)

While Yahweh's command to Jonah was not exactly evange-listic in nature, it clearly reveals that His heart has always been set on seeking those who are otherwise positioned to receive divine judgment. He has always placed priority on extending mercy to the lost.

But let's be honest—most of us don't make this much of a priority ourselves. Not in practice anyway.

Now wait! Don't skip this chapter. I know you might be tempted, but hang in there with me because this is important. I don't want you to miss one of the critical messages of Jonah.

The first memorable word in the "Great Commission" (as Matt. 28:19–20 is commonly known) is "go." Our old grammar teacher would've called this verb an imperative, a command, But it's actually not a command at all. In the Greek language the word translated "go" is an aorist participle. It could literally be trans-lated "going." In other words, making disciples is something a believer does while "going" about the business of the day.

So while nothing is wrong and everything is right with wide-spread evangelism efforts being organized and spearheaded and staffed with volunteers, this is not the only way (or even the pri-mary way) for believers to obey this word from Jesus. Declaring the message of God's love for the lost is not just something to do; it's a way to live.

And basically, we don't.

I came across a little booklet called *The Sin of Silence* by William Fay, a Southern Baptist evangelist who equips people with the passion and tools to share Christ with others. He cites some statistics from his own denomination that reveal how far down the priority ladder our concern for others' eternal destiny has fallen. In one recent year, for example, a third of its churches welcomed no new believers into their fellowship. *Not one!* Another third of churches baptized six people or fewer. And perhaps the most shocking number of all: the estimated percentage of Christians who will go to their graves without *once* telling another person how they can be saved through Christ Jesus—97.4 percent. That's almost everybody.

"These aren't just black-and-white numbers to me," he writes. "These are real. These statistics walk around in church clothes and do church things. They sing in the choir and pass the offering plates. They help out in the kitchen and take turns in the nursery. They do many, many wonderful things for the cause and kingdom of Christ. But there's one thing they don't do. And won't do. Ever. Maybe not even if their lives depended on it. *They will not bear witness for Christ.*"[17]

Oh, we're glad when the pastor does it. We think it's great when we hear a guy like Head Welch giving his testimony on television. But as far as one of us being personally involved in the spiritual transformation of someone else's life, it might never cross our minds in a million years. Why do we feel this way?

Well, lest we think we're unaffected by what's taught in the halls of academia, including our Bible schools and seminaries, the reality is this: philosophies and worldviews shape cultures. Ideas matter. And one of the ideologies in recent history that has trickled down into our thinking is what's commonly known as "process theology," part of which maintains that God, rather than being completely "the same yesterday and today and forever" (Heb 13:8), is changed by and adaptable to things that happen in the world. In other words, an issue that might have held great importance to Him at one time in human history may not matter as much to Him now as it used to.

We shake our churchgoing heads in disgust at such an audacious claim. But don't the findings reported by Mr. Fay and others, as well as the known extent of our own evangelistic inactivity, tell us we're living as though Christ's instruction about "[going] therefore and [making] disciples" (Matt. 28:19) is not what it was once cracked up to be?

I can certainly think of times when I've barricaded myself behind the protection of sleep or reading on an airplane rather than engaging the person next to me in conversation, even if they were the type who wanted to talk. I can think of times when I shied away from injecting spiritual matters into a discussion for fear I might stick out and sound silly. Most memorably, I can think of the many times I passed up an opportunity to talk about Jesus with a woman who lived on our street, only to hear an ambulance racing into our neighborhood early one morning to come to her aid. They were too late.

So was I.

If this sounds like the same old guilt trip you've heard a hundred times before, let me remind you that the call of Jesus to go and make disciples is no less clear and binding on us than God's call for Jonah to go to Nineveh. And running from Him in this critical area out of fear or doubt or whatever justification we choose will invariably result in a level of self-imposed distance and dryness in our relationship. He does not take His Word to us any more lightly than He did with Jonah. We know how *that* went down. And we should expect more of the same ourselves as long as we, too, keep running from this paramount responsibility.

No one's condemning you here. This is merely our Father's loving correction and discipline at work in our lives. By His grace today we have a second chance to act in obedience and start this over.

Because so many others need their second chance.

—— Under the Anointing ——

As the curtain began rising on Jonah's first day of prophesying in Nineveh, we can only imagine the panic he must have been feeling inside. Palpable fear and intimidation. Isn't that what keeps most of us from being quick and free to talk about our Christian life with unbelievers? Afraid to offend. Afraid of their reaction. Afraid we'll be asked something we don't know how to answer.

For a public speaker, one additional fear is typically dumped into the mix—a fear I know all too well. The night before a conference or teaching event, even though I'm typically assured I'll be addressing a receptive audience, and even though I've prepared long and hard to determine what I'm going to say, I lie awake in bed trying to gauge whether I've got too much material in one spot and too little in another, whether I'm liable to run long or—worse—run short, run out. One of the most frightening things God can do to a speaker is give him or her a message to declare that doesn't fill up the allotted time.

But that's the kind of message Jonah got. He had been told in Joppa, you remember, to be standing by for God to deliver his note cards to him. And when they finally arrived, the whole message could have fit on a Post-It note.

> Yet forty days and Nineveh will
> be overthrown. (Jon. 3:4)

That was it.

In the Hebrew langauge, this sentence is a grand total of five words—no illustrations, no funny stories, no icebreakers to butter up the audience. Just a little bitty message. Heavy on judgment and light on personality.

Yet it was a message that would stir unprecedented, house-by-house repentance in a pagan city.

See, I've sat in places where a preacher went on for hours and no one was touched. Yet here's Jonah, uttering five words that God gave him to speak in an extremely hostile environment, and the whole place responded—by the hundreds of thousands.

> The people of Nineveh believed in God;
> and they called a fast and put on sackcloth from
> the greatest to the least of them. When the word
> reached the king of Nineveh, he arose from his throne,
> laid aside his robe from him, covered himself with
> sackcloth and sat on the ashes. (vv. 5–6)

That's the difference between having *words* to say and having *God's* words to say. The difference between operating under your own steam and operating with God's anointing, with His presence, power, and favor circulating through you. And that's what we have available to us when our hearts are fully yielded to His interruption, when everything about us just does what He says—even if it's stopping in the mad dash of running our errands to notice a person who's tearing up in the greeting card aisle. You're not following a program or flipping into witnessing mode. You're just obeying. You're just caring. You just know that Jesus is everybody's answer for everything.

And you walk over with God's anointing.

This is why we can yield to this as a way of life because it's God doing the work through us, not only in sharing the hope of Christ with an unsaved person but in performing any of those small, simple acts of obedience that comprise every aspect of your life.

It may be just an apology extended to your spouse, but God's stamp of anointing on those few words can set off ripple effects in your marriage for years to come.

It may be just a simple meal, either bought or prepared for a person in need, but God's stamp of anointing on those few little items can speak His love and comfort to much more than some-one's stomach.

It may be just five dollars placed in a person's hand or a couple of quarters inserted into their parking meter, but God's stamp of anointing can turn your simple gift into a treasure that reaps an eternal return on your meager investment.

A creek behind our house is just a small, gentle, peaceful little wading brook—most of the time. But the day someone decided to drain a nearby pond into the waterway upstream from us, the mouth of that creek turned into a rushing river. By the time it spilled over hills, down paths, under roads, and around other peo-ple's properties, eventually reaching the area behind our house, the water level of our slender creek had risen into what looked like a diving pool in the backyard. It was beautiful! Someone had created a small change in the water source miles away from us, and the impact was felt by dozens of homes and families down the line, including ours.

It's like the widow at Zarephath giving a small loaf of bread to the prophet Elijah, which God transformed into a never-ending supply of good eats for her family the rest of their days. It's like Esther bravely approaching the king, then seeing her entire race spared from a conspirator's plot. It's like Ruth obeying the simple instructions of her mother-in-law, going into the field of Boaz to glean, and unknowingly entering the family lineage that would birth the great King David and ultimately a humble man named Joseph, stepfather to the Messiah.

The results of your simple obedience, when infused with God's anointing, can produce results you never imagined. What He does with the prayers and Scriptures you invest in your chil-dren can create spiritual giants for the generations to come. What He does through the phone call you make or the letter you write to a discouraged friend could spark a revival in their soul that never goes out. Even the few simple words of Jonah's message, filled with God's anointing, were enough to cause the king himself—yes, the wicked king of hostile, hated Nineveh—to get up from his throne, take off his royal garments, and stand in repentant sackcloth and ashes before the Lord.

There's power in God's anointing.

And those who yield to divine interventions can count on it. This is not about preaching on street corners. It's about letting what God inserts into your life—whatever it is, wherever it happens—become an opportunity for obedience, as well as an opportunity for Him to turn a small thing into a truly mind-blowing thing.

I'm telling you, I not only want God's presence *in* me; I want His presence *on* me. There's a difference, you know. I want more than realizing He is merely in me; I want my life to be a living witness and window to His grace and glory—without even saying a word. I want people to sense the peace of God when I walk into a room. When they enter my home, I want them to be immediately aware that this is a place where God hangs out. When you and I just roll with His plans for us, we can expect to be the simple instrument His Spirit uses to do all kinds of marvelous things, including drawing others to Himself.

If you've ever heard author and lecturer Elisabeth Elliot speak, you know she's the type of communicator who gets right to the point. She doesn't doll up her talks with a lot of fluff or filler. She just brings the Word, teaches the Bible. A friend of mine, Cheryl, who has gone to hear Miss Elisabeth teach on numerous occasions has actually developed a personal friendship with her—close enough that when they crossed paths at another women's retreat once, they made plans to have lunch. And during the course of their time together, Cheryl brought up this point to Elisabeth, asking—just wondering—why she didn't bother herself with warming up an audience or telling a lot of personal stories, choosing instead to jump right into the meat of her topic without serving up any appetizers first.

Cheryl said Elisabeth looked back at her almost confused by the question and, after a few silent, quizzical seconds, said, "Now why in the world would I want to do that, to tell stories? People don't come to see *me*. They come to see *God*."

Wow.

What if we truly lived like that? What if we entered into each moment of life knowing that everywhere we go and everything we do, our purpose is for people to see God in us, to sense His presence, to be drawn toward His Spirit at work in our smile and posture and handshake and greeting. We can't change people's lives, but God can. We can't make a lot of difference, but God can. We don't have much important to say, but God does. And it doesn't take Him long to say it when His presence and anointing are on us, when obedience to Him defines the way we make every next choice. What Jonah experienced in Nineveh could be what we experience as well in our own little corner of the world, watching God take one little act of basic obedience and transform it into something He can use to turn a person's whole life around.

When I was fourteen, I went with my aunt to a local Christian bookstore to take sign language lessons, studying under a spunky young woman who was adept in the art of signing. Her skill, however, went much deeper than her applied training and knowledge. She possessed a true heart for God and a desire to see lives changed through this ministry craft.

I remember her telling of a time when she was relatively new to learning sign language, sitting in a worship service where God's Spirit was moving in a tangible, powerful way. The preacher was delivering a passionate message on salvation, and people were responding by the handful. Our teacher looked up in the midst of this spiritually charged atmosphere, happening to notice a small group of deaf visitors who were in church on that occasion. And her heart began aching for them to hear the Word being shared.

But she hardly knew any signs. She was nowhere near capable of translating everything the pastor was saying, certainly not at the speed he was traveling. Grappling with what to do, she stood up quietly and slipped over to where these people were sitting, looked them squarely in the eye, and signed four simple words she knew how to communicate: "Jesus. Died. For. You."

Within a matter of minutes, tears began flowing from their eyes. Each of them flooded to the altar without prompting. Four simple signs, employed with only an amateur's ability, had been infused by the anointing of God to work wonders in people's hearts.

When we respond to our second chances by obeying Him with new determination, entirety, and abandon, His Word and work can do amazing things through us, enough to spill over into second chances for lots of others.

—— How Is This Happening? ——

I remember as a little girl being stunned and shocked by several things about Jonah's story, not the least of which was the immediate, overwhelming conviction that spread like wildfire through an entire city of people. Even as an adult, I've wondered, *How'd that happen? How could one simple five-word message create that kind of impact?*

Let's consider several things. First of all, remember that Jonah had spent three days and nights in the stomach of a big fish. That's bound to have left a scar or two. You know what it's like to be sensitive and not want to be seen because of a bad haircut, or a face blemish, or a stain on your outfit. Jonah would've given anything for that to be the worst of his problems.

I found one other instance, from 1926, of a man who was swallowed by a huge shark while fishing in the English Channel. Two days after this tragic incident, the fish was sighted and killed. When they opened the shark's body, they found the man inside, unconscious but still alive. He was devoid of all hair. Yellow and brown splotches were recognizable all over his skin due to his interaction with a toxic mixture of gastric fluids. The stench emanating from his body was staggering, nauseating.[18]

While we don't know the extent of Jonah's injuries or how impaired his appearance was when he arrived in Nineveh (especially considering he'd traversed five hundred miles to get there), he could hardly have been the picture of health as he traipsed through the streets and side yards of the city. His 8 x 10 glossies wouldn't have gotten him a preaching gig anywhere on the planet.

And yet when Jonah splashed through town in obedience to the word of the Lord, the result was a "fishers of men" haul of amazing proportions. It wasn't as though only a few folks from one isolated community believed in God or a handful of the city's most important people. Every citizen of Nineveh "from the greatest to the least" immediately responded. Incredible.

Conviction was so complete, in fact, that even the animals were made to participate in the governmentally mandated fast.

> Both man and beast must be covered
> with sackcloth; and let men call on God
> earnestly that each may turn from his
> wicked way and from the violence which
> is in his hands. (Jon. 3:8)

It was stunning. Amazing. "Even the great apostle Paul never experienced anything comparable to what Jonah saw. Paul never saw an entire city turned to God."[19] Would Jonah's message have been this impactful without the scars of his past rebellion and consequences clinging to him? We don't know. But surely part of what triggered this stunning revival was that Jonah seemed to the listening Ninevites like someone who'd been resurrected from death.

God was obviously up to something supernatural.

Here's something else: in 765 BC, and again a few years later in 759, two different plagues ravaged the city and environs of Nineveh. Disease and sickness swept through the region, killing many. Up until this time Nineveh's walls and ramparts had always been considered an unassailable protection from enemy attack, but not even this ancient superpower city could erect a garrison strong enough to ward off the horrors of blight and intestinal invasion. "These plagues, coupled with a total eclipse of the sun in 763 BC, were enough to soften the Ninevites to Jonah's preaching."[20] Prior to Jonah's arrival God had already been at work to prepare the ears of the people in Nineveh to be receptive to His word through the prophet. Each of these disastrous events, which Jonah may have known nothing about, would have left an odious environment in the city that left the Ninevites eager to seek a solution.

God was obviously up to something supernatural.

Jonah's little part was just to obey. To say his five little words and move on. To do what God had told him to do. God would take care of the big ol' rest. And when He does that—when His anointing and presence sweep through the clear passage created by our simple obedience—then our little lives, our sluggish words, our awkward attempts and wordless hugs turn into something we never dreamed possible.

Supernatural, in fact.

Second chances start happening all around us.

Why? Because He has gone before us, orchestrating our pasts and our present condition (both good and bad), using circumstances to cultivate the hearts of people long before we get there so that ultimate impact can be made. When we obey, we are doing nothing more than entering a set of circumstances that have already been divinely placed in motion long before we arrived. It's a divine setup.

And to God be all glory.

— So Go to Nineveh —

"To go to Nineveh," writes author James Limburg, "means for us to let the great needs and the great instances of evil in the world completely determine the best direction of our efforts and lifework."[21] Nineveh, we know, was a "great city . . . an *exceedingly great city*," filled with "great" opportunities for God's mercy and restoration to flow. The Ninevites needed a second chance, as do many who are around you today. You can look about you and see pockets of "exceedingly great" spiritual need—in your children, in your family, in your city, in your area.

God will show you where the needs are, and He'll show up before you can even get there, preparing the way for your arrival. This is still what takes priority to Him. And He will let you know which ones He's called you to be available for, the places where He intends to touch others' lives through your available, obedient heart. You can't reach them all by yourself. You're not supposed to. That's what the church is here for, to unite believers across all races, backgrounds, and doctrinal stripes into fulfilling the Great Commission command of Christ Jesus. But our tall, personal stack of second chance receipts still demands that we go where God is calling us.

"Jonah was not supposed to go to the whole world," Limburg says. "'Go to Nineveh!' Go to the one place whose great needs God has opened your eyes to see. Risk your life and prepare yourself to do that which the Lord commands. Jonah was, after all, an individual."[22]

Like we are.

Individuals with second chances. People who know what God has done for us, and who know what His grace and saving power can do for others. So we obey. And obey. We make this our ongoing habit and pattern: *to obey*. Then God translates our troubling interruption—His mighty, divine intervention—into a holy strength that not only picks us up in the morning but, by His presence and anointing, also snatches up people in our homes and streets and towns and train stations who are desperate for the same second chances we got.

Go to Nineveh, Jonah. And proclaim His message.

And expect something supernatural to happen.

Part 5

Unfinished Business

CHAPTER 13

God on Our Own Terms

When God saw their deeds, that they turned from their wicked way, then God relented concerning the calamity which He had declared He would bring upon them. And He did not do it. But it greatly displeased Jonah and he became angry.

JONAH 3:10–4:1

I love to hear the grunts and giggles of my little Shirer boys when they're down on the floor horseplaying with their daddy. Love those fun, familiar yet (I know) all-too-fleeting moments when we're all here at home together, when the day's winding down— this precious season of life when the house is so full of energy and vitality. It's like music to cook dinner by.

But sometimes when they roll around and raise the roof with their muscular play, testing out their young testosterone against a guy more than twice their height and strength, a bit of frustration can set in for them. It's all fun and games, you know, until somebody gets hurt or doesn't feel like they're winning.

Like the day our five-year-old came stomping into the kitchen, his little arms crossed hard in front of his body, his bottom lip poking out. Jerry had apparently thrown down one of his trademark wrestling moves and had pinned our son in a position he couldn't wriggle out of. Made him mad.

"Mom," he pouted, "I'm not playing with Daddy anymore, and I'm not talking to him either. He's not playing fair."

What do I look like, a referee? In fact, I tried not to laugh out loud at his cute display of aggravation. But this was serious business to him, and I knew I needed to step in to help if I could. So I knelt down beside him, gathered him up on my knee, and asked him if he knew how big and strong his father was. "Yes," he snapped, "and I'm not talking to him any more today!"

"But, son, what about those times when he's the only one around here who's big and strong enough to fix things, and lift things, and carry things? Aren't you glad to have a daddy who's able to do stuff like that for you *then*?"

See, my little boy had forgotten for a second that he couldn't just accept all the helpful, beneficial, feel-good aspects of his dad's nature, then get upset when Jerry used that same power in a way that didn't suit or please him.

"Be Dad on *my* terms," he was essentially saying.

Jonah would be a case in point of this. A short while after finishing all the preaching required of him in Nineveh, he positioned himself at a remote location outside of town "until he could see what would happen in the city" (Jon. 4:5). But even before observing the outcome, he had already started to get ticked all over again—mad that he had been brought here, mad that these people still seemed to matter to God, mad that in all likelihood, since these rank heathens had repented, they would fall on God's available mercy extended toward them.

Jonah? Mad? Are you serious?

He seemed to have come so far in the short time we've known him. The heaven-sent storm and the living submarine ride had appeared to produce a positive effect in his life, resulting in a noticeable change of course and some good exit poll numbers coming out of his preaching tour in Nineveh, indicating that his message had been well received. That should've pleased him, right? I know when I prayerfully put together and deliver a message as a Bible teacher, I'm hoping more than anything that it will penetrate the hearts of each listener and bring about a genuine life change. I not only want them to hear it; I want them to respond to it. You'd think that's how *anyone* would feel.

But this is Jonah we're dealing with here—a man who loved God but still seemed to love his own way a bit more. And while his sense of displeasure could perhaps have been sparked by any number of factors stemming from his time in Nineveh, one thing we know for sure is that he was not happy with God's desire to show mercy toward Israel's enemies (even though Jonah dearly loved the way God showed mercy toward him and his fellow Hebrews). He hoped his message had fallen flat and that God would end up flattening Nineveh after all. That'd show 'em.

Again, this surprises us a bit in Jonah, but it probably shouldn't. Is it possible there are characteristics of God you appreciate when they're beneficial to you but secretly despise when they're at work in the lives of someone you're not too fond of? Like maybe an ex-spouse or boyfriend who betrayed you? Maybe that person who stole from you or cheated you? Maybe that parent or relative who perpetrated some heart-rending offense against you? Though you may have tried to forgive, is it arguable that you'd still find a level of satisfaction in seeing God punish them severely for what they've done, never again extending favor toward them the rest of their lives? We like what God's grace does for *us* but not always so much what it might do for a few others we could name.

In other words, we want God to be God on our own terms. *This*, but not that. *Here*, but not there. *Now*, but not then.

Let's wrestle, but let me win.

But that's not the way He works.

— Who Knows? —

God, you see, is always eager to extend mercy and compassion. This is true to His nature, consistent with His heart's desire. So when He "relented concerning the calamity which He had declared He would bring upon" the Ninevites (3:10), He was merely acting in accordance with His very being and purpose.

Granted, from the outside looking in, He seemed to be breaking His own rules. Hadn't He declared in His Word that He was not One to "change His mind" (1 Sam. 15:29; Ps. 110:4), the way we humans are so prone to do? Yet when we read this event, He certainly appears to be flip-flopping as a result of something He saw happening in Nineveh. He had said He was going to destroy them, but He didn't.

Even my boys noticed this when I read them the third chapter of Jonah. They couldn't see how the all-knowing, all-powerful God I'd been telling them about could make a decision to do something—"Yet forty days and Nineveh will be overthrown"—and then decide to do something different. If He knew what He wanted to do, seems like God would *just do it*. Regardless.

Actually, though, He'd done this before. Centuries earlier He seemed to let Moses talk Him into giving the children of Israel another chance after their sorry, outrageous display with the golden calf. "The LORD changed His mind about the harm which He said He would do to His people" (Exod. 32:14). He later heeded an appeal from the prophet Amos and called off a locust infestation He had sent. "The LORD changed His mind about this" (Amos 7:3). He commanded Jeremiah to stand and speak His word to the people in the temple, thinking "perhaps they will listen and everyone will turn from his evil way, that I may repent of the calamity which I am planning to do to them because of the evil of their deeds" (Jer. 26:3).

But this "repenting" is different from what humans do when we feel sorry about our sin and wish to put it behind us. In the Hebrew language, "the word most frequently employed to indicate man's repentance is *shub*, meaning 'to turn' from sin to God."[23] This is what the Ninevites had done by responding to the Lord's message of judgment through Jonah. They had turned away from their sin and wickedness. God, however, is completely free from sin, so the idea of "repenting" doesn't apply to Him. The word for this action in reference to God is a different one— *nacham*—which means "to be moved with pity."[24] See, it's not as though God had made a mistake or was trying to correct an error. He hadn't actually changed. He *can't* change. It's contrary to His nature. But *Nineveh* had changed. And that brought out something consistent with God's nature: His quickness to respond to man's repentance.

Saying that God "repented" or "relented" is the same as saying God *responded*. He saw an entire people group expressing sadness and grief over their sins, and He did what God always does when even one tired, sickened sinner recognizes his life is a mess because of it.

God responds. He shows mercy.

If that wasn't His heart, there'd have been no reason to announce that judgment was coming in "forty days" (Jon. 3:4). The city's destruction could've come by nightfall or at high noon or right that second—without any advance warning. They certainly deserved it.

But God wanted to show mercy, not judgment. That's His heart. That's His nature.

And the king of Nineveh must have picked up on this caveat. This is why he wisely suggested that the whole city begin to fast and pray. For "who knows," he said, "God may turn and relent and withdraw His burning anger so that we will not perish" (v. 9).

"Who knows . . ."

Unaware of whether Jonah's message constituted a conditional pronouncement or an unconditional decree, the king prefaced his statement with a "who knows." He didn't attempt to assume or arrogantly suggest that automatic forgiveness would fall from heaven because of his and his people's change in attitude. Like the prophet Joel calling the children of God to repent— "Who knows whether He will not turn and relent and leave a blessing behind Him" (Joel 2:14). Like King David praying and fasting for the recovery of his dying son— "Who knows, the LORD may be gracious to me, that the child may live" (2 Sam. 12:22). We need to be people who leave room for "who knows" in our walk with the Lord.

Will God always call off judgment? Will He miraculously change the situation you're currently facing? Will that lost loved one of yours finally see Him clearly and receive His boundless mercy for their sins?

Who knows?

I don't. Neither do you.

But God knows. And knowing that He longs to be gracious and compassionate should be just what we need to keep us on our knees, even when we're entering the most hopeless of situations. Unless, like Jonah, that's a side of God's character you don't want to share with just anybody.

— Faithful and True —

You know how it is when we get mad—sometimes we start mouthing off. We say things we don't mean, even though our words may be telling and descriptive about what's really happening inside our hearts. Sometimes when we're alone and needing to vent, we'll even address our heated grievances in God's general direction—toward the interior roof of the car, for example, or the ceiling over our bed. It can be some of the most honest "praying" we ever do.

That's what the Bible calls Jonah's rantings in chapter 4 of his Old Testament book. A prayer.

> He prayed to the LORD and said, "Please LORD, was not
> this what I said while I was still in my own country?
> Therefore in order to forestall this I fled to Tarshish, for
> I knew that You are a gracious and compassionate God,
> slow to anger and abundant in lovingkindness, and one
> who relents concerning calamity. . . . than life." (vv. 2–3)

Sounds like Jonah knew a lot about God. Not surprising, his being a prophet and all. This particular litany of divine characteristics was drawn from a core teaching of Hebrew doctrine appearing multiple times in the Scriptures, but first revealed to Moses when he brought to the Lord a new, second set of stone tablets on which He was to write the Ten Commandments again. Coming down around Moses in a cloud of glory at this holy moment, God declared Himself to be "compassionate and gracious, slow to anger, and abounding in lovingkindness and truth" (Exod. 34:6).

Interesting, Jonah left out that last part about God's abounding in "truth"—and I don't think it was because he couldn't remember the whole verse word for word. Possibly, he'd conveniently left out something that didn't help to sell his side of the story. He glossed over a "truth" about God's character that runs from one end of Scripture to another—that He never changes or wavers or becomes false to His nature. You and I do not get to decide what we want to be true about God in certain seasons of life and then true about Him in others. He stays steady and faithful and true whether we like it or not, whether it's convenient to us or not, whether it meets with our approval or not. We must take God with an as-is sticker on Him. No return policy. We must accept both Him and His ways fully and completely, from beginning to end.

Maybe, like Jonah, your beef with God is that someone else is getting (or has gotten) a seeming "break" you don't think they deserve. And you're mad that He's treated this particular person with a measure of grace or favor or patience or prosperity you don't think rightfully belongs to him or her, not the way it belongs to you. You're like the older brother to the prodigal son, sulking and perturbed that the mercy, kindness, and blessings of God are not limited to people like yourself.

You want Him to do things your way, on your terms.

Or maybe you're at a place right now where you're not happy with the way God's treating *you*. You think you deserve better after all you've done and been for Him. You don't understand why He's withholding a desire of yours from you, or placing an unwanted burden on you, or pressuring you so intensely during a period of life when you just really need to rest and recoup.

You want Him to do things *your* way, on *your* terms.

Maybe you've sort of made a deal with God. You'll yield to Him, you'll go along with what He's telling you to do, but on the back end you're expecting a guaranteed return on your investment. It's true, of course, that the Bible contains many, many promises we can take to the bank, assurances of God's peace and contentment and abundance of life, but we are masters sometimes at trying to force conditions on God that we consider to be anticipated paybacks for services rendered. We feel like we have the right to haggle with Him, see if we can talk Him into a bargain at a price we're willing to pay. Otherwise, we might just walk.

It's like those shops I love so much where you can pick up a bracelet or purse with a sticker price of thirty-five dollars, then tell them you'll take it for twenty. Thirty, they counter. How about twenty-five? You meet somewhere in the middle.

Might work at the flea market but not with God.

I've got to be honest with you: if you choose to yield, surrender, and be obedient to Him, things may *still* not go the way you were hoping, the way you thought He'd respond to your part of the deal. We must always leave room for God to be God—on *His* terms, not ours. He is operating in our lives with a kingdom agenda that is so much bigger and grander and longer lasting than whether or not He's satisfying us on this particular Saturday afternoon. He is wisely, sovereignly, lovingly orchestrating plans and purposes that leap generational lines, cross geographical boundaries, stuff we could never wrap our minds around. And for us to think this is some kind of cosmic Monopoly board where we can box Him into trading our three railroads for His Boardwalk is arrogant and out of bounds.

Jonah-like.

God is not cavalierly dismissing your concerns and your genuine needs, but He may express His love and kindness toward you in ways that won't seem like it until you look back ten years from now—or in ways you may *never* understand until you're worshipping Him in glory. But you've got to trust that your God is "righteous in all His ways and kind in all His deeds" (Ps. 145:17), that He knows the plans He has in mind for you, "plans for welfare and not for calamity to give you a future and a hope" (Jer. 29:11), that He is fully capable of being God and is extremely good at His job.

We receive so many calls and e-mails and blog responses at our ministry from people asking, "Why?"—why is this happening to me, why would God allow such a thing, why would He expect me to endure this? Like the woman I heard from recently, a single mother of four. She's had her heart broken by a husband who left her, as well as a broken engagement with a man who changed his mind at the last minute. Both of these men have moved on now. They're married with families and seem to be thriving. But not her. She's struggling to make ends meet, trying to take care of her family, and feeling a bit lonely in the process. This wasn't the way things were supposed to work out.

It's not hard to see where the questions come from. And I'm so glad you're willing to share your hearts with us as you grapple with them. The reason folks like us can hurt and pray with you is because every one of us has asked some of these same questions ourselves, just as David, the psalmists, and the prophets so often lamented in Scripture, even the Lord Jesus on the eve of His trial and crucifixion, "My God, My God, why have You forsaken Me?" (Matt. 27:46). But there are some things we just don't and can't know. Some of the answers we seek are wisely and sovereignly hidden in the mysteries of God. And bottom line—for you, for me, for everyone who claims the name of Christ through faith in the grace of God—we must cling with an iron grip to His living Word that assures us our victorious Lord "is called Faithful and True" (Rev. 19:11).

Our God—Jonah's God—is not only great, He is also gracious. He is not only ours, He is also redemptively inclined toward all who stand in need of hope, forgiveness, and a second chance, whether we think He should or not. Our anger toward Him is distracted energy that, if turned into trust and surrender and confidence in His omniscient purposes, would assure us the ongoing blessings of relationship with the One whose Word stands forever, the only One who can keep *us* standing on either end of a life interrupted.

— Why So Angry? —

When I approached the fourth chapter of Jonah in preparation for writing and study, Jerry and I were in a stretch of life where an important decision was needing to be made concerning one of our sons. We had talked and prayed and tried hashing this whole thing out, looking at it from all angles, and let's just say we weren't in total agreement on which way to go. We were in what I often call "heated fellowship" with one another—not quite an argument but far from a calm conversation.

I knew that Jerry was going to have the final say-so on this. And because I was fairly certain which way he was leaning, my blood was already beginning to boil. I was already feeling resentful and cross, and he hadn't even made the decision yet. I'd already mapped out how many days I planned not to speak to him, how I was going to do everything I could to make his life as miserable as possible. (Don't look at me like you don't know what I'm talking about.) I was going to be upset, and believe you me, he was not going to have to read between the lines on my forehead to know it.

Then along came God's Word.

Interrupted by Jonah yet again.

Now before I tell you the exact verse God's Spirit used to speak personally to me on this occasion, I want you to know this: When ancient Israel read aloud the book of Jonah, the end of the prophet's opening tirade in chapter 4 would be punctuated by a noticeable pause. The Masoretic text, one of the oldest and most reliable Old Testament manuscripts, includes a *setumah* in that location, a grammatical device that indicates a slight break or breath in the reading.[25] This pause would have placed emphasis on the piercing response given by God. When I consider that, I can't help but think of a parent listening and waiting and tapping his foot until his whiny child has finally gotten out all his sad little complaints and has settled down a bit. Then after a pause, filled only with one cleansing sigh of silence, he bends over, eyeball to eyeball with his little one, and responds with all the patience and authority he can muster.

So try putting yourself in God's shoes, listening to the prophet's temper tantrum. Read Jonah's comments. Then pause. Finally, slowly and emphatically read God's response.

Jonah: "Please, LORD, was not this what I said while I was still in my own country? Therefore, in order to forestall this I fled to Tarshish. . . . Therefore now, O LORD, please take my life from me, for death is better to me than life" (vv. 2–3).

[Pause]

God: "Do you have good reason to be angry?" (v. 4).

That question. It must have hung in the air over Jonah for a moment as the gravity of it sunk in. God's questions seem to do just that.

You see, He has a real knack for asking questions, especially ones for which He already has the answer. Think Adam and Eve in the garden (Gen. 3:6–11), Cain after his brother Abel's murder (Gen. 4:3–7), Philip and the other disciples standing around with five loaves and two fish and five thousand empty mouths to feed (John 6:5–6). I'll have you know that this ancient question of God's to Jonah became modern-day for me as the Spirit turned its spotlight my direction. It was one of those moments when, after reading a portion of Scripture, you actually sit up and look around in all directions because you think God might actually be standing behind the curtains or over by the closet.

"Priscilla," He seemed to be saying to me, "I've not only got *your* life, but the life of your children, your husband, your family, your future grandchildren, all in the palm of My hand. I am sitting on the throne supervising it all. And have I not always taken care of you even when things didn't go the way you preferred? Jerry may be making the decision on this, but as always, I'm the ultimate decision maker. I am here, taking care of this, and I know what I'm doing. Do you really have a reason to be angry after all I've done by way of provision, protection, and keeping My promises in your life?"

He asked it of Jonah.

He asked it of me.

Now He's asking you.

"Do you have good reason?"

Actually, from a purely human perspective, Jonah had all kinds of reasons for being upset and would continue to have reasons in the days to come. In 722 BC, "approximately thirty-eight years after Jonah preached to Nineveh, the army of Assyria pillaged the Kingdom of Northern Israel, laid seige to Samaria, and dragged every last citizen into captivity."[26] Their usual method was to consume entire civilizations by intermingling with the captured people groups and erasing their national identities. The northern kingdom of Israel was basically lost to history from that moment on, and Jonah had Nineveh to thank for it—the place where he had gone to declare God's great, compassionate interest in them. He probably felt a fair share of blame for his role in keeping their city's prospects afloat.

Of course, Jonah was mad. Who wouldn't be?

So I don't want you to hear me saying that your circumstance or interruption is not severe and impossibly complex, that no one could possibly fathom why you're making such a big deal about it. Believe you me, the situation between Jerry and me was intense enough to drive even my closest girlfriends to their knees on my behalf. It's understandable that tears come to your eyes as you grapple with this, and that anger can easily seethe to the surface, that it's making your life terribly difficult right now. But because God is the One in control because He is much more experienced and adept than you are to handle this matter in the way a totally perfect Father would care for His child, and because you know beyond any doubt that He loves you and can work all things together for your ultimate benefit, "Do you have good reason to be angry?"

Really?

In Jonah's case God was working out His divine purposes, mysterious and incomprehensible as they may have seemed. And it really wasn't Jonah's business to tell God what to do or how to act or to shake a scolding finger in His face and call Him a traitor. It wasn't *Jonah's* place, and it's not ours either.

You may be in the midst of a circumstance right now that's got you upset. You're frustrated; angry about the outcome God has allowed. You're unsure why this is happening, perhaps not at all in agreement with how God is choosing to handle it, knowing He could do anything He wanted and make this immediately better and resolved. Instead He seems content to keep asking questions and addressing your heart motives rather than just fixing what's broken or out of balance.

But He doesn't ask us these hard, challenging questions just to hear Himself speak. He already knows what the answer is. His goal in posing such a question is to help us come around to agreeing with Him on the answer, unearthing the inner issues we didn't even know were down there, giving us an opportunity to relinquish our claw grip on control and anger so that we can rest in the blessed assurance Christ died to give us. He knows there are more important things to result from this interruption than a conclusion—things like a heart at peace with His holy will, trusting in His wise counsel, believing in His goodness, surrendering to His purposes even when we don't like them or don't understand.

We think we know what we want. In reality we should want nothing else but to be completely in line with His desires for us and His purposes in our generation. So we must resolve to let God be God on His terms, not ours.

A while back Jerry and I were getting dressed to go out fancy, just the two of us, and I had gotten a new outfit to wear for the occasion. I was feeling pretty good about it—you know, when you finish adding a touch of makeup and take those last few pats at your hair, when you look and turn and angle yourself in the mirror and decide, "Yeah, that looks nice."

Sweeping into the other room where my husband was waiting, I gave him the eyes that asked, "Well, what do you think?" And being the honest, objective, lucky-he's-still-alive kind of guy I love and married, he said rather matter-of-factly, "I don't really like that shirt."

And I didn't really like that comment.

Poor man. Jerry didn't know I'd already written a script for how this little interaction was supposed to go. I was supposed to look beautiful, and he was supposed to tell me so. But when we've written a script that the other person hasn't seen or known about, one that's all been composed in our own head, we can't really expect or force them to read their lines the way we wrote them.

But we do that with God far too often, like Jonah did. We tell Him how things are supposed to go. We tell Him what we're wanting to happen. We tell Him what our will involves in this particular situation. And then we expect Him (if He loves us) to sign off on the script we've written. After all, we've put this outfit together from head to toe, and all we need is His blessing and approval. Then we're all set to go.

Enter anger. Enter silent treatments. Enter childish decisions not to speak to, pray to, or have anything else to do with Him until He comes around to seeing things more in line with our perspective, until He does something appropriately judgmental toward the people we're most angry with. And as sad and unattractive as it looks on Jonah, it looks the same on us.

"Do you have good reason to be angry?" Not if you know what's really good for you. Not if you know how deeply in need everyone is, even those you don't really care about.

Not if you really know who your great big God is.

CHAPTER 14

The Many Moods of Jonah

So the LORD God appointed a plant and it grew up over Jonah to be a shade over his head to deliver him from his discomfort. And Jonah was extremely happy about the plant. But God appointed a worm when dawn came the next day and it attacked the plant and it withered.

JONAH 4:6–7

We had a recent winter in Dallas that was one for the record books. Lots of cold weather. Lots of thick, wet, deep, beautiful snow. Thank the Lord for digital cameras because I don't think there was enough Kodak film at any drug store within driving distance that could've kept us amply supplied. (Not sure there was any laundry detergent left in town either after all of us moms washed the mountains of wet play clothes piled up on our back steps.) Nobody wanted to miss even one minute of this rare Texas snowfall.

We were like kids on a carousel. It was so much fun. But not so much on the ninth or tenth consecutive day of freezing temperatures when the propane tank in our yard ran out of heating fuel, leaving us with a cold house, a nonworking stove, and no hot water.

Good feeling gone.

I can't tell you how glad I was to hear the gas man knock on our door one chilly afternoon around 4:30 to spare me another day of depending on the radiated heat from my laptop to keep me semiwarm in my sweat suit and plush, woolly robe while I was writing. Within minutes I cranked up that thermostat as high as it'd go and quickly began defrosting myself under the vent in our bedroom ceiling. Ahhh . . . heat. Bliss.

Come on, springtime.

We can be real creatures of comfort sometimes, can't we? If it rains too much, we gripe about having to slosh out to the grocery store with our umbrella again or about the kids being cooped up inside with all that tightly wound energy. If it doesn't rain *enough*, we moan about how hot it's been and what the drought has done to our front lawns and potted plants. Air on, heat up, our pillows fluffed just right, our favorite snacks in the pantry—it can often take a lot to keep us from getting grouchy.

Seems like a fitting place and mood for us to catch up with Jonah following his time spent in Nineveh after he'd broken off negotiations with God, not even bothering to answer His question about anger, making a beeline out of town like a sullen two-year-old.

Having all four chapters laid out before us as we do, we possess insight about Jonah's situation that he did not. He wasn't certain yet what God's decision toward Nineveh would be, so he'd located a spot far enough out of fire-and-brimstone range where he could watch the explosive proceedings of Nineveh's downfall with his feet up. "Yet forty days and Nineveh will be overthrown," God had inspired him to say to these savages (Jon. 3:4). *Overthrown*. It was the same odious, devastating word used in Genesis 19:25 to describe God's annihilation of Sodom and Gomorrah. The word meant utter ruin and destruction.

Perched there on the outskirts of Nineveh, he erected some sort of shelter from which he could view the fireworks he hoped would still fall—most likely something with walls but with nothing more than a leafy roof, affording him little protection from the sun's glaring rays. It probably got pretty toasty in there as the day wore on—an appropriate temperature to match the red heat underneath his own collar from having done what he'd done and seen what he'd seen. This divine intervention had just been too much for Jonah to handle. Hanging around Nineveh had felt as creepy as he'd thought it would. His anger over what his enemy's repentance might mean in the big picture had pushed him so far, he was at least toying with the idea of suicide. That's how deeply this cord of Ninevite discord ran within his Hebrew blood.

And yet one simple change in his climate-control situation was about to brighten his mood considerably. In a matter of moments, Jonah would soon be switching from complete despair to joyous enthusiasm.

—— Plants, People, and Priorities ——

> The LORD God appointed a plant and it
> grew up over Jonah to be a shade over his head
> to deliver him from his discomfort. And Jonah
> was extremely happy about the plant. (Jon. 4:6)

Think of it. The possibility that an entire city full of people might be rescued from sin and peril had made Jonah want to die. Yet the sudden appearance of an overhead shade plant was oddly exciting enough to snap him out of a horribly morose mood and set him on a new emotional path. Made him happy.

No, not just happy. "Extremely happy."

Now who am I to judge poor Jonah? I've already admitted that a newly filled tank of heating fuel and the prospect of boiling some water on the stove for tea had the innate ability to fire new hope back into my shivering soul. I was more excited about our restored climate-control conditions than just about anything else that could've happened to me that day.

Being too hard on myself, you think? Too picky? Nothing wrong with being cool about my toes being warm? I hear you. But if we're listening closely enough, divine interventions have an uncanny way of giving us key warnings about the state of our hearts. Interruptions, even the positive ones, can often reveal some hidden, deceptive imbalances that could cause us trouble later on if left undiagnosed and untreated. It's like noticing your car's not braking well, or is idling a little rough, or is leaving some oil stains in the driveway. They're small signs that a tune-up is in order. For Jonah all the signs were pointing in this direction. The problem wasn't that he was enjoying the plant; nothing wrong with that. The problem was that he cared more about a plant than people.

Consider this. Jonah viewed the intensity of his "discomfort" in the sweltering heat (v. 6) as being of similar magnitude with the "calamity" from which God had spared the repentant Ninevites (3:10). The noun translated as both words is precisely the same in the original language. This obvious overexaggeration of Jonah's own trouble and hardship shows us something worth noting and should've shown it to him too. His internal measuring system was skewed toward reading his personal pain with a hyperinflated sensitivity, while being fairly immune to others' suffering and grief.

That's a problem. Needs realigning.

Also, you'd think God's compassionate gift of shade would've compelled Jonah to want to "comfort those who are in any affliction with the comfort with which we ourselves are comforted by God" (2 Cor. 1:4). This touch of supernatural relief from the torrid heat should have triggered a sense of discernment in him, the kind that might've helped him be at least a little more sensitive and welcoming to the grace and kindness being offered by God to the Ninevites. The Lord had once again shown divine favor to Jonah, and yet Jonah remained as resistant as ever to seeing what an equal gift God's deliverance would be to others.

That's a problem. Needs realigning.

And we're no different. We, too, often require the ongoing maintenance of God's interventions to help us recognize not just the obvious villains like anger and pride and more traditional pockets of sinfulness but also other things that are misaligned, those inner issues that can be somewhat harder to detect. Like a judgmental spirit. An unhealthy absorption with self. Lack of sensitivity toward other people's needs. Unwillingness to be inconvenienced. Little things that hinder us from letting God's plans, priorities, and activities be of foremost importance to us.

We need to know when this is happening. We need to be told when there's an inconsistency between our character and God's. We need to be shown how little regard we can sometimes have— by contrast—for the deeper, more important, more substantial matters that supremely interest His heart.

There's nothing like spending a little time in God's garage to get us spiritually roadworthy again. His interventions may cost us a bit more than we were hoping to pay, but the rewards of driving at top performance can take a lot of the worries out of life as the road rolls along. God's divinely scheduled tune-ups can mean less sluggishness in the curves and gear changes, as well as fewer stops for unnecessary repairs down the line.

And Jonah's tune-up was scheduled to begin. Right . . . now.

> God appointed a worm when dawn came the
> next day and it attacked the plant and it withered.
> When the sun came up God appointed a scorching east
> wind, and the sun beat down on Jonah's head so that he
> became faint and begged with all his soul to die, saying,
> "Death is better to me than life." (Jon. 4:7–8)

As quickly as Jonah's comfortable shade plant had appeared, it was gone. And with the hot sun bearing down on him again, boosted by the added exhaust of a "scorching east wind," God chose this opportune moment to ask a question that would've sounded familiar to Jonah—"Do you have good reason to be angry about the plant?" (v. 9). The first time God had asked a question like this (v. 4), He had focused on Jonah's anger toward the larger issue of Nineveh and God's decision to show mercy toward its people. His second question focused more narrowly on this solitary plant and Jonah's anger toward the loss of it. Like a small child needing to have a problem broken down for him into its simplest parts in an attempt to help him understand, Jonah was getting an elementary lesson on God's priorities.

The first time Jonah had no answer. This second time, he peppered his response with what was most likely "a Hebrew expletive."[27] *Yes, Lord,* "I have good reason to be angry, even to death" (v. 9). Apparently he still wasn't getting the message. God cared intently about sinful, hurting, broken people; Jonah cared disproportionately about a stupid little plant, enough to want to die because of what it had meant to him.

That's a problem. Needs realigning.

Clearly, then, the Ninevites were not the only ones in this story needing an adjustment in their attitudes and behaviors. Jonah, too—the prophet of God—possessed a heart and mind in great need of being reset. He was overdue for a repositioning of his priorities.

So this is a good time to ask: Have your divine interventions, along with the lessons learned from watching Jonah, uncovered some clogged arteries in your thinking system, some habitual ways of responding to life that are out of phase with the way God looks at things?

- Are there, for instance, some "plants" you're more concerned about than the people and plans God has put before you to care for; some enjoyments and living conditions you will not do without, at least not without a fight and a real sense of feeling deprived?
- Are you willing to extend grace to others in the same measure it's been extended to you, even if it's toward that person who routinely frustrates you with their demands or their nagging?
- Do you overexaggerate simple inconveniences in your own life so they begin to seem as overwhelming and devastating as others' calamities or the stake of their eternal destiny?
- As you consider God's long-suffering and compassionate way with you, are you willing to tear down your touchy, unbreachable wall of hardness toward anyone who makes you feel betrayed, belittled, or just ignored in some way?
- Does your personal pain and loss prevent you from recognizing the hurt and need that exists around you in others' lives—troubles you could seek to alleviate or at least offer your comfort and encouragement regarding, allowing your own experiences to help you relate to what they're going through and to lift their spirits?
- Are you more enthusiastic about the season finale of your favorite television program or the opening weekend of March Madness than you are about people's lives being changed by the liberating power of God's grace?

I know these are hard questions, some of them *particularly* hard considering the life experiences that have helped to forge each situation they bring to mind. But God is asking, and we need to answer.

If ignored or faced with resistance, these dilemmas come with the ongoing potential of keeping you from following Christ with your whole being, the way you've always wanted to. And they will continue to keep your relationship with Him strained and unsatisfying if you choose not to deal with them. They will leave you feeling spiritually barricaded from living with tangible purpose and meaning.

They're problems. And they need realigning.

—— Consider the Source ——

I hope you've noticed that the chapters of this book have been purposely divided into five sections, tracking the major life changes of Jonah's story (and ours). I've called this final section "Unfinished Business" because we can obviously see that Jonah, while making a few minor strides in the obedience department throughout his biblical ordeal, quickly experienced some major lapses in chapter 4 that revealed a need for additional tweaks and do-overs. God had used some simple yet powerful, life-sized illustrations to show Jonah he was due for a tune-up. And we can all learn a lot from them.

I'm sure you've been where Jonah was. You may be there now—worn out and miserable and tired of being asked to give so much—until you don't know if you can put up with any more. Everything was piling up on him. Jonah reached this point in his recorded life story completely in despair. The same root word that describes how feverishly the worm "attacked" Jonah's plant and destroyed it (v. 7) is the same one used in verse 8 "to indicate the burden of the hot sun."[28] He didn't see how he was going to make it through this. Like you sometimes, he probably felt like he was under a curse. Emotionally spent. Physically drained. Nothing was going his way.

But while Jonah wasn't happy at the time with all these issues in his life, they were precisely what he needed to help him see the disparity between his religion and his reality. And no one knew what he needed more than God did. I wonder if Jonah made the connection between his difficulties and God's hand? Possibly he was so disheveled and disgruntled by his lot that he didn't even notice the divine lessons Yahweh was seeking to teach.

These corrective measures had been carefully crafted by God:

- The plant in verse 6 had grown to the precise height of Jonah's little makeshift shelter, sturdy enough to give him sufficient shading.
- Likewise, any number of wild animals could've caused Jonah life-threatening trouble while he was camped there on the outskirts of town all by himself, yet God allowed only a little worm to come along, an insect that could specifically harm his plant.
- God didn't send a blast of searing wind from any random direction but sent it specifically from the "east" (v. 8). Since Jonah was already "east" of the city walls (v. 5), he wouldn't have the benefit of being shielded from the wind by the walls, as he might if he were on the other side.

Of course, not every difficulty in your life is directly sent from God. Though nothing can reach you that He doesn't allow, we must exercise discernment and ask for His wisdom in knowing if it's something we should pray against (like an outright enemy attack), or if it's been specifically crafted and is the Lord's way of spurring us onward in our walk with Him. Tough spiritual decisions, these. But we never go wrong in the face of even a maddening interruption to turn our eyes to the heavens, eager to see what He may be trying to accomplish in us, aware that we often fail to recognize and consider His participation in life's events.

I believe one of the ways should cause us to consider that God is behind the events in our lives is when we can't pinpoint any other source, when there's nothing in plain view we can identify as the culprit, nor a solution to patch up the problem. In Jonah's case, while we don't know the exact type of plant that God had given, the worm probably attacked at its base. It's plausible that from Jonah's perspective, the plant just began to wither without any noticeable explanation. It would've been hard enough to deal with his shade source was wilting away, but not being able to figure out why or do anything about it would have made it utterly frustrating.

Have you experienced a few disappointments recently, and you can't seem to pinpoint the source of the problem? Could they be His plan to get you around to some unfinished business you need to deal with? Think about it.

This may not be the best time to say it, but it's true just the same: difficulties are to be expected. And yet because these interruptions are much more than they seem—because God employs or allows them as *divine interventions*—they truly are instruments of ultimate blessing.

You've just gotta believe that.

— A Better Way Forward —

While Jonah responded to God's questions with stiff-arm resistance, we can learn from his mistakes and choose not to make the same ones. We can consider our interruptions a good time to invite God in to work on what needs fixing. We can thank Him and His divine interventions for helping us spot our weak spots before they get any worse, before they lower our gas mileage any further and keep costing us more every day—much more than we realize over the course of our lives. And we can trust the indwelling Holy Spirit not only to start tinkering and repairing but to change the way we do things.

See, when God uses corrective interruptions to help us realize the gap between our character and His, we're not left on our own to complete the connection. We have His Holy Spirit within us not only for companionship and comfort and counsel and guidance but also for empowerment—His surpassing, seemingly impossible empowerment. And while we'll never yield to Him perfectly enough to get this totally right, we can deliberately choose to grow each day, perfecting our willingness to surrender and to let Him do His heroic work through us.

It's not called the "fruit of the Spirit" for nothing (Gal. 5:22). Love and kindness and self-control and all the rest supernaturally start growing in us as we daily, consistently yield to His authority, laying down our own ability to accomplish anything spiritually significant or successful on our own yet fully—and I mean *fully*—trusting that He can do it through us, through our submitted hearts. God's Spirit really is enough. He's *more* than enough. Nothing that stands between you and the person God's Word is calling you to be is powerful enough to withstand the power of the indwelling Holy Spirit.

The reason grace and forgiveness and compassion and long-suffering are expected of us is because these are the things that matter most to the heart of God. And when our hearts more closely resemble His in ever-increasing fashion, we begin participating with Him in daily tasks and long-term activities that make our safe, sensitive, self-centered ways as abhorrent to us as they once were appealing.

Wonder what would happen if instead of saying no and turning away, we truly listened to whatever God has been exposing to us in the midst of our interrupted lives, the specific areas where His Spirit has pointed out our need to yield to Him more completely? What would happen if the things that were of primary significance to Him became the same things that were of most significance to us?

Like Jonah we've got some unfinished business to tend to.

What do you say we get up and get with it?

CHAPTER 15

There's So Much More to Tell

You have heard; look at all this. And you, will you not declare it? I proclaim to you new things from this time, even hidden things which you have not known.

ISAIAH 48:6

I went to see a movie with a couple of girlfriends the other night. We sat there the whole time completely riveted by the unexpected plot surprises. We shed a few tears at certain spots along the way, totally enthralled in the experience—so moving and touching. Then as we began to sense the two hours nearing their end, as the storyline felt like it was beginning to wrap up, it just . . .

Didn't.

It just quit. The screen faded to black, the credits began to roll, and it was over. Just like that. People sitting around us gathered up their things and started to leave, but none of the three of us moved a muscle. We just stared silently ahead, then turned and stared at each other with blank expressions. Our jaws hung open in disbelief.

Was that it?

Hey. Wait. We still had several questions that weren't answered. Loose ends that hadn't been tied up. Issues that were left dangling out there, begging for closure. How could we have sat there for so long, wrapped up so tightly in this thing, only to leave disappointed and unsatisfied?

As we reach the end of the book of Jonah, that same sense may come rolling over you. I wish I could tell you that his story closes with a bang and a neat, tidy conclusion, but that's just not the way it is. There's no march across the parted waters of the Jordan into the Promised Land. No grand reversal of misfortunes like we find at the end of Job's dramatic ordeal. No redemption-in-the-end scenario like the scorned little brother Joseph, extending blessing and forgiveness to his undeserving brothers. No grand celebration of return as the prodigal son's father runs to greet his boy on the road home.

No closure.

No final good-bye.

No epic finale.

Nope. None of that stuff here. The last verse of the last chapter of Jonah ends with a question mark. And appropriately so because that's where the questions really begin.

Where does Jonah go from here? Is this the start of a change in his character, or does he slink back into rebellion and resistance? Do the Ninevites come out of town looking for him, curious to learn more about this Hebrew guy who'd created such a revolution? Does he dare try to go back home, fearing what his people might do to him for betraying their loyalty? Does he ever make it to Jerusalem to offer those sacrifices he'd mentioned in the fish's belly? Or—what I really hope for—does he live to face the divine interventions in his future with a different perspective, with a willingness to surrender to God's plans?

Kinda hate leaving him here like this.

Kinda hate him leaving us here like this.

No production theater would make a play with so obscure an ending. No publishing company in the world would accept this manuscript and put it in print. Despite all the action and intrigue and interesting setups, the payoff simply isn't there.

Nevertheless, our *God* has decided to put it in print. With a wisdom far greater than any review board or literary critic, He has preserved this important account down through the ages from one person's true-life experience to ours. Therefore, while we may be tempted to feel frustrated over the things we're not told, perhaps we should take a second look and focus on what we *are* told. For when we do, we'll find that Jonah's story leaves us with much to celebrate, ponder, and incorporate into our own lives.

—— In the End ——

This entire narrative began with "the word of the LORD" (1:1). And in the end, God's word brings it to a close.

In the last few verses of Jonah, God speaks more extensively than He's spoken in the rest of the book put together, peppering His words with comments and questions designed to pierce the prophet to the core, intending to make an impact on both his heart and his mind.

> You had compassion on the plant for which you
> did not work and which you did not cause to grow,
> which came up overnight and perished overnight.
> Should I not have compassion on Nineveh, the great
> city in which there are more than 120,000 persons
> who do not know the difference between their right
> and left hand, as well as many animals? (4:10–11)

And just like that, the story ends with God's comments and questions lingering there in the air. Unanswered. Open-ended.

Not exactly what we expected. Not only does it feel incomplete; it sounds sort of . . . testy. After hearing the moaning prophet wishing he was dead rather than having to put up with all his "problems" (v. 9), we'd like to think the next scene might've been something equivalent to God the Father sitting down beside him, patting him encouragingly on the back, empathizing, consoling, even agreeing with him that He knew these interruptions had been demanding and hard on him—poor Jonah, having to go through so much.

Yet our wise heavenly Father seems to have taken a much different tone. He implies with His holy sentiments that the prophet would do well to consider his own humble position in relation to that of God's loftier one. "I am God," Yahweh basically asserts. "I've brought into existence all the things you've ever enjoyed, including this plant you're so upset about losing. So as much as I love you Jonah, you're out of place to question what I do with these things or how I determine to use them. I'm in control around here, not you."

It's reminiscent of the Lord's approach with Job, remember? After his story begins with a rapid-fire description of Job's many setbacks and tragedies, the first thirty-odd chapters of his book are largely taken up with grumbling, complaining, and people telling Job what he's supposed to think. A few high moments of faith and perseverance are sprinkled around, but also a lot of hand-wringing and fairly overt anger with God for allowing these things to happen with no real hint of explanation.

Not until near the end of this whole account does God speak up—primarily, again, with questions, such as these for Job to answer: "Where were you when I created the earth? Tell me, since you know so much! Who decided on its size? Certainly you'll know that! Who came up with the blueprints and measurements?" (38:4–5 *The Message*). "Who took charge of the ocean when it gushed forth like a baby from the womb? That was me! I wrapped it in soft clouds, and tucked it in safely at night. Then, I made a playpen so it couldn't run loose" (vv. 8–10 *The Message*).

And God was just warming up. Did Job know how to awaken the dawn, how to locate the storage facilities where the hail and snow were kept? Did he know how to tip over the water jars of heaven to send rain on the earth, or how to make sure the young lions have all the food they need? Who did he think had scooped out the earth's canyons, or arranged the stars in their heavenly places, or designed the stately prowess of a horse in full gallop? "Speak up if you have even the beginning of an answer" (v. 18 *The Message*).

This goes on for verse after verse—one imponderable mystery after another—until God sums it all up in chapter 40 by saying, "Now what do you have to say for yourself? Are you going to haul me, the Mighty One, into court and press charges?" (v. 1 *The Message*). *Do you really expect to have the last word on this, Job? Do you still believe you know as much as you think? Do you actually feel like you have the right to know why I do what I do?*

Good questions.

Not just for Job.

Not just for Jonah.

More importantly, for us.

Do we have the right to be upset about the loss of shade from a withered plant we had no part in creating or even cultivating? Do we purport to know how God is supposed to conduct His business or feel He owes us an explanation for every action that falls outside our preferred set of options? How dare we think for a moment that we know better than God, unwilling for Him to keep us in the dark as to why this interruption has entered our lives in this way, at this time, with this cost, for this long? Why don't we realize that by demanding to understand what's going on, or by thinking we deserve an answer, we're attempting to put ourselves in a position above and ahead of God, treating Him as though He's obligated to honor our requests for information or relief if He chooses not to give them? We're relegating Him to the position of a cosmic bellhop, ready to jump at our beck and call and submit to our every whim.

Don't you see that when it comes to jockeying with God, He wins by a "knows"? He has all the answers? He remains in charge? He keeps being God even when you'd like Him to explain Himself, even when you feel it's important for Him to hear how you'd do things differently if you were running the show?

Now please hear me clearly: God cared for Jonah. And God cares for you too. He's not a hard-nosed parent waiting for any opportunity to wag His finger in your face. No, there's grace in His eyes. Care and comfort drip from his lips, even as He speaks with the kind of directness that brings us much-needed discipline and conviction.

But don't confuse His Father's heart with fun and games. He knows when He needs to throw His weight around. He knows when the most loving gesture of all is the one that puts us in our place, the place where real surrender can begin.

— Positive Developments —

God's exertion of authority and privilege is what gives this ending to Jonah's book its power. But the sweet, profound beauty of this inconclusive conclusion is found simply in God's spoken word being given to a runaway, rebellious prophet—a man who definitely would have been on the bad side of most others by now. God is not *coddling* Jonah, obviously, but check this out: He's not *ignoring* him either. The fact that the God of the universe would go out of His way to shed light on His thoughts is entirely overwhelming. While His initial goal in utilizing the plant, worm, wind, and sun may have been to illuminate and expose Jonah's off-base *priorities*, now He desires to give His child a shift in *perspective*.

Toward *God's* perspective.

See, God doesn't use His vaunted position over us merely to sling out orders and commands. Rather, His desire is to mold the hearts of His children, bringing us around to His eternally true and accurate way of thinking. This wasn't just a divine diatribe; it was a pure teaching moment intended to give divine insight and perception to someone who didn't really deserve to have it.

Someone like us.

Can you believe it? As for me, I can barely stand it—the thought of God wanting to go out of His way to expound His perspective on life's situations. While He has every right to leave us to our own limited, human viewpoints, paralyzed with dread as we stare blankly out the window of our lives, trying desperately to escape the uncertainty of the interruptions we face, He chooses to fit us with spiritual vision so we can see things as He sees them and thus feel compelled to surrender ourselves to Him more completely.

And I'm going to go out on a limb here. I'm going to say Jonah got it. I think he walked away from this four-chapter drama with a changed mind-set. Why? Because if he hadn't, I don't think he would've let his book end like this. Doesn't sound like the Jonah we've come to know.

Whether or not he is the author of his own story is an issue widely debated among scholars. But I believe he is, as do many respected commentators. And that means he chose under the inspiration of God's Spirit to conclude the retelling of his story in this most inconclusive way. He obviously considered these brief thoughts and questions of God to be a fitting ending to his legacy, letting God have the last word. In the end Jonah was willing to tell a personally revealing, self-effacing story of his own rebellion, not making himself the hero or actively justifying his behavior, even in the big wrap-up. Only a humble and transparent person could do such a thing. Rather than wanting no one ever to hear the seamy details, holing himself away in bitter isolation and dis-illusionment the rest of his days, he chose to be clear about what happened to him, beginning right from the start. And right from the start, the truth didn't make him look too good.

- *Chapter 1.* God called for a storm to intervene in Jonah's life, and it came and went at God's appointment. Even polytheistic sailors responded to God's activity.
- *Chapter 2.* God called for the big fish, which swam to the specific coordinates of Jonah's wind-tossed ship, then spit him out three days later at the exact spot where God commanded it to.
- *Chapter 3.* An entire city of Hebrew-hating pagans turned away from their wickedness and received God's undeserved mercy. Even the king himself submitted himself to an extreme, repentant fast.
- *Chapter 4.* The plant, the worm, the sun, and the east wind arrived right on the dot, doing precisely what God had assigned them to do.

The only character in this whole account who was rarely *where* he was supposed to be, *when* he was supposed to be there, *doing* what God wanted him to do . . . was Jonah. The preacher. Turns out the one in the story who needed the most transformation of all was Jonah himself.

Jonah's story narrative makes a clear point: sometimes God's people are the most in need of being changed and molded by His expert shaping tools. Sometimes we're the ones who most need to get our heads screwed on right, to get our perspectives cleared up. And Jonah wanted to make sure in these final, pertinent verses that we didn't miss this point completely, just in case it hadn't sunk in during the first three and a half chapters.

Who knows but whether this one spot—this pivotal moment when the Lord left a question echoing in Jonah's mind—was where God's divine perspective on the plant, the Ninevites, and this whole set of events finally took root in Jonah's heart, causing him to put ink to scroll and record his dramatic saga. Could this unsatisfactory ending actually be a literary clue to us that the most important thing Jonah wanted to say is what God had said to him at this one historic time and place, just east of an enemy city? In hearing the Lord take this blunt tone of voice, maybe Jonah finally grasped what God had been trying to get through to Him all along.

Interruptions call for surrender.

And when we do, the supernatural effects can be mind-blowing.

Perhaps this is where you and I can realize it too. Perhaps here at the end of *this* book is where we can begin to realize that the rigid-sounding response of God to Jonah came with a matching piece of encouragement. In the same way that God's all-consuming knowledge and power keep you in your rightful, humble place before Him, they also exude confidence that He's got your back. The life interruption you're facing can be seen and accepted as a divine intervention simply because He's behind it all and continues to control it all. You may be surprised by what's happened, but He's not. You can rest easy knowing He's looking after your well-being. If He has the boundless capacity and bandwidth to handle all this information and insight concerning you, concerning me, concerning everybody we know, then He's got more than enough divine muscle—not to mention enough faithful, covenant love—to stay in complete control of everything that's happening to you, even if you don't know exactly what it is, even if you don't see any good reason for Him having you here.

So Jonah . . . just relax. He is and has always been on His job. You may not *get* to know what's behind all this, but that's OK because you don't *have* to know. All you need is the perspective that knows your God is at the wheel, setting you up to be the key player in an enormously supernatural outcome that is beyond what you'd ever expect.

— Will We or Won't We? —

My friend Brigette called me the other day with bad news. Breast cancer. None of us knows what all this is going to mean. We're certainly praying for a miracle, asking God for complete healing, either through the immediate, overnight elimination of these harmful cells or through the medical treatments already prescribed to deal with her condition.

She's been taken aback, yes. There's shock in her voice.

But I'll tell you what else is there. Brigette can't wait to see what God is going to do with this. She is actually, honestly looking forward to walking faithfully through this trial, this adventure, fully trusting that God is offering her opportunities to serve Him in ways she'd never have had the privilege of participating otherwise.

Here's a woman who hasn't just been *living* through her life interruptions but *learning* from them. Here's someone who's not depending on a favorable outcome or a five-page explanation before journeying ahead with God toward whatever He has in mind for the next, unexpected phase of her life. Here's a person who's walking ahead with spiritual eyesight—with God's viewpoint and perspective—with a heart molded to accept this as a divine intervention that promises who knows what kind of spiritual wonders and possibilities along the way.

And to hear her talk like that, I can't help but be inspired and encouraged.

You may say, "Oh, she's just in denial. Wait till the full weight of this kicks in. She'll be singing a sadder, much more realistic tune a few months from now." Sure, there may be some low days to come for Brigette. She may wake up some mornings wishing her name never had the word *cancer* attached to it.

But that doesn't make the depth of her trust, obedience, and surrender any less genuine or detached from reality. Hers is the confidence that's truly available to every child of God, every day of the week, through every interruption that's either currently on your plate or distantly on the horizon.

Brigette doesn't know what to expect. But she knows she can just surrender to it. She can trust the One who is calling her here. He's inviting her into something supernatural.

That's what we can expect from divine interventions.

Whether or not Jonah ever came to terms with this we can't *really* know. God has chosen not to tell us. But I guess our not knowing about Jonah's response isn't really the issue here. The big question to ask at this moment is not, "What did *Jonah* do?" but, "What will *we* do?"

What will *you* do?

- Will you begin recognizing that your life interruptions are actually divine interventions, calling you to treat them differently from before?
- Will you yield to God's instructions instead of running off in the opposite direction?
- Will you surrender your plans and purposes into the greater known of God's unknown designs for your life?
- Will you listen for His call to relationship even when the

path to deeper intimacy feels frightening, risky, boring, or unpleasant?

- Will you be more willing to seek out the "Ninevites" around you, offering them the same mercy your God has extended to you?
- Will you continue clinging to comforts and entitlements even when you know they're hindering more than they're helping?
- Will you follow? Will you trust Him? Will you just obey . . . anyway?

I've gotten over the disappointment that Jonah's story seems to stop in midsentence without any real resolution. But with the final line of his story leaving us in mystery, and much of our own story still unknown to us, there's one thing we can know for certain: yielded, obedient surrender will keep us right where God wants us. It will enable us to see our lives and futures the way God sees them, approaching each day with His contented, confident, comforting sense of perspective. Choosing to yield in obedience to His wise direction and calling is how a lot of our unfinished spiritual business becomes constructed into a legacy of faith. More each day. Each time we trust and obey.

—— God Only Knows ——

I can say it now: Jonah's story hasn't let me down—even with the wrap-up that never really wraps up. In the end I can walk away with this stirring notion: the interruption Jonah tried his hardest to run away from was an opportunity to be part of the *greatest revival in human history.*

Pretty stark when you put it *that* way.

God was offering him a grand prize, and all he could see were the problems. Yet that is exactly what God is offering us—a better way, His perfect will, a key role in His flawless plan for the ages. But here's the rub: it may be wrapped in the cloak of an interruption we can't make out, and our tendency is to run away from it. We might even be able to say, as a rule of thumb, that the greater our desire to run the other way from an interruption, the more substantial the outcome God is preparing to bring about. Doesn't it stand to reason that our enemy—the all-star running coach—would want us out on that track every second if something eternally spectacular might arise from our going God's way instead?

We just don't know what God is brewing. We just need to follow Him while fully trusting Him.

I'm so glad Jude led me to Jonah. That sweet, cuddly, two-year-old wad of energy has taught me the lesson of a lifetime. Oh, sure, the idea of having a family of five at this crazy-busy time of life took some real getting used to. And, yes, we've each had to adjust our living space, reorganize our schedules, shift our plans around, and reorchestrate our habits as a result. Divine interventions often require that. But the power of God's perspective made clear by His closing words to Jonah have opened my eyes to something I might never have seen clearly otherwise.

You see, the summer after Jerry and I were married, we attended one of his family reunions. Sometime during that day, one of his cousins walked over to us and, in the course of a brief conversation, said something that rocked my husband to the core: "Jerry, did you know you're the last man to carry on the Shirer name?" Sure enough, a glance around the backyard filled with relatives clarified this as fact. Jerry was indeed the final opportunity for this name to continue. And as this particular relative excused herself from where we were sitting and filtered away into the crowd, Jerry just sat there, not saying anything.

After many silent moments, he turned to me, eyes filled with emotion, as the enormity of what he was sensing brimmed to the surface. He pulled me aside and explained that there were men in his family who'd not been faithful to the Lord. He could recall his mama more than once being down on her knees, crying out to God, asking that any generational curses be broken and that her children would pursue a way of life that honored Him.

"Priscilla," he whispered in such a hushed tone, I had to lean in close to hear him clearly, "I really think the Lord's intention is to do something afresh and anew with us, with you and me. I feel fairly certain in this moment that He is commissioning us to be a part of it by rearing godly Shirer men."

This was coming from someplace deep inside. This was God doing business. This was special. I knew it, I could sense it, and I've never forgotten what Jerry said next: "Priscilla, when we have children, I believe the Lord will give us all boys."

And now, eleven years later, that's just what He's done. When I look at my three sons, new perspective intact, I see divine intervention at work—allowing us, if we'll fully surrender and engage in this all too fleeting season, an opportunity to participate with Him in one of the most sensational and stirring opportunities of my entire life. He's giving me the chance to rear some young warriors for Christ Jesus who are going to leave my nest one day and take up the fight in their generation. I'm sitting on the edge of my seat, chin nestled in my hands, to see what God is going to do.

With my children.

With my husband.

With me—a regular, everyday woman choosing to surrender to a life interrupted.

Your details are different. Your interruption—personal and unique. And yet what's required of you is the same thing required of me: surrender. It's the only thing that can help us navigate the unexpected. I'm learning that it's worth it, and I hope you'll join Jonah and me on this journey.

The rest of your story is yet to be written. The pen of heaven is waiting. God's Spirit is exuding inspiration, courage, and perspective.

Onward, modern-day Jonah.

The best is yet to come.

Notes

1. J. Vernon McGee, *Jonah: Dead or Alive?* (Pasadena, CA: Thru the Bible Books, 1984), 13.

2. John H. Walton, *Jonah, Bible Study Commentary* (Grand Rapids, MI: Zondervan, 1982), 13.

3. McGee, *Jonah: Dead or Alive?*, 13.

4. Hal Seed, *Jonah: Responding to God in All the Right Ways* (Oceanside, CA: New Song Press, 2008), 31.

5. Walton, *Jonah, Bible Study Commentary*, 14.

6. McGee, *Jonah: Dead or Alive?*, 13.

7. *A Walk Thru the Book of Jonah* (Grand Rapids, MI: Baker Books, 2009), 11.

8. Seed, *Jonah: Responding to God in All the Right Ways*, 33.

9. James D. Devine, *A Journey with Jonah to Find God's Will for You* (Glendale, CA: Regal Books, 1977), 31.

10. James Limburg, *Jonah: A Commentary* (Louisville, KY: Westminster/Knox Press, 1993), 49.

11. See http://www.desiringgod.org/ResourceLibrary/Sermons/ByDate/1982/367_Cry_of_Distress_and_Voice_of_Thanks, accessed June 3, 2010.

12. Limburg, *Jonah: A Commentary*, 70.

13. Ibid., 72.

14. Walton, *Jonah, Bible Study Commentary*, 35.

15. Devine, *A Journey with Jonah to Find God's Will for You*, 109.

16. Seed, *Jonah: Responding to God in All the Right Ways*, 76.

17. William Fay, *The Sin of Silence* (Nashville: Holman Bible Outreach, 2010), 5.

18. See http://www.thruthebible.org/site/c.irLMKXPGLsF/b.5706581, accessed June 3, 2010.

19. McGee, *Jonah: Dead or Alive?*, 34.

20. Seed, *Jonah: Responding to God in All the Right Ways*, 78.

21. Limburg, *Jonah: A Commentary*, 76.

22. Ibid., 77.

23. R. Laird Harris, Gleason L. Archer Jr., Bruce K. Waltke, *Theological Wordbook of the Old Testament* (Chicago: Moody Press, 1980), 1344.

24. Joyce Baldwin, *The Minor Prophets: An Exegetical and Explanatory Commentary* (Grand Rapids, MI: Baker Books, 1993), 581.

25. Limburg, *Jonah: A Commentary*, 93.

26. Seed, *Jonah: Responding to God in All the Right Ways*, 108.

27. Walton, *Jonah, Bible Study Commentary*, 60.

28. Devine, *A Journey with Jonah to Find God's Will for You*, 149.

My hope is that you'll walk away from the pages of this book with a different perspective on life's interruptions. As we've seen with the prophet Jonah, they can be surprising divine interventions. There are so many similarities between us and Jonah, between his story and ours. I have no doubt that the more deeply you dig into his life, the more clearly you'll see your own life and circumstances. I've written a Bible Study to help you do this. We've included a sample from the seven-week study for you to get started on this journey.

Blessings,
Priscilla

JONAH

Navigating a Life Interrupted

Sample Chapter

PRISCILLA SHIRER

I AM JONAH

I Am Jonah

*"The word of the LORD came to Jonah the
son of Amittai saying." Jonah 1:1*

I am Jonah.
I want to serve God …
    as long as it is convenient.
I desire to do His will …
    until it is a tad uncomfortable.
I want to hear His Word …
    as long as its message is one I'm supposed
    to pass on to someone else.
I don't want to have my plans interrupted.
Oh yes. I am Jonah, and I suspect that in
    one way or another, you are too.

The story of Jonah has been a tale too extravagant and too outlandish for many people to believe as truth. They can't wrap their minds around the storm, the big fish, the city's revival, the sun, the east wind, and the plant that all play a role in this compelling narrative.

Were it not for my own firm belief in the inerrancy and validity of Scripture, I might doubt its veracity as well. Yet with all its unique qualities, I am drawn to the prophet and his true-life saga for one critical reason: Jonah was the only prophet who ever ran from God. I can relate to that. When my life and plans have been interrupted, I've wanted to rebel against it.

Have your life plans ever been interrupted?
◯ yes ◯ no ◯ not sure

Have you ever run from God? ◯ yes ◯ no ◯ not sure
Write your thoughts.

If you answered yes to either of these questions, Jonah's story is your story.

I hate to be interrupted!
Say it with me now:
"I HATE TO BE INTERRUPTED."

Yesterday I had a chance to relax for two hours. It was a delightful surprise to come across some quiet moments alone. I don't know how it happened, but Jerry ended up out of the house with all three of our little boys.

Yes, Lord!

Those two hours became precious to me. I became intent on guarding them. Anything that might invade my treasured plan to relax was overlooked to the best of my abilities. I didn't want to be disturbed.

You know the feeling, don't you? The disgust and overwhelming frustration that washes over you when you are derailed off your chosen course for your day or even the one free hour you surprisingly come across. If you do, then you can also imagine the compounded frustration of having a life that's been interrupted. We planned one thing for our lives, and yet our current situation looks nothing like what we had in mind. Someone tampered with our ambitions, goals, and dreams. The yellow-brick road of our lives veered off in some unexpected direction.

What are some of your life goals that you've yet to see become a reality?

How has life tampered with those goals?

Some changes we're delighted with. Others disappoint us and leave us buried in questions. Without a firm belief in the goodness and the care of God, we can spend years mad at ourselves, mad at others, or even mad at Him because we didn't get to accomplish what we originally set out to do.

In the margin list three adjectives that describe how you feel about interruptions you've faced in your life plans.

Often we equate the term *interruption* with upheaval, derailing, and frustration. Who wouldn't try to avoid those? Yet a closer look reveals an issue of value. When we deem our current task as an essential priority, we'll look with contempt on anything that threatens our time focused on it. Why? We've given priority and credited value to the current task, person, or goal.

We learn about Jonah's priorities in 2 Kings 14:25, the only other time he is mentioned in the Old Testament.

According to 2 Kings 14:25, what was Jonah's job?

Was he successful at his job, and how did you determine your answer?

As a prophet to the Northern Kingdom of Israel, Jonah's priorities would have included:
1. hearing from God
2. declaring God's messages to His people
3. being identified as a true prophet of God

I believe God and His will held prominent importance to Jonah. He loved his people and wanted to see them rise in power and influence. It seems Jonah likely enjoyed success because what he prophesied was happening.

From your personal goals you wrote, would you say you gave highest importance to God and His will?

During the reign of King Jeroboam II, the nation's territories that had been taken by Syria were restored. While we know little of Jonah's life prior to the events in the chapters we're studying, we do know he had foretold these good things for his people. As a result he most likely was popular, highly respected, and appreciated. In addition, he probably enjoyed financial security.

Read Jonah 1:3. What might this verse reveal about Jonah's financial security?

Jonah lived in a time of national economic prosperity. Israel regained lost territories and achieved its most prosperous time since Solomon. Israel's wealth exploded because it controlled important trade routes

"[King Jeroboam] restored the border of Israel from the entrance of Hamath as far as the Sea of the Arabah, according to the word of the LORD, the God of Israel, which He spoke through His servant Jonah the son of Amittai, the prophet who was of Gath-hepher."
2 Kings 14:25

through Palestine that connected the ancient world. In fact, some rabbinic commentators think the Hebrew text implies Jonah chartered the entire ship, cargo and all.[1] If so, he must have had adequate financial means.

According to Jonah 1:1, Jonah's interruption began when "The word of the LORD came" to him. His priorities and life of comfort were disrupted with directives that would put him in an entirely new and different direction than that which he was currently enjoying.

> What do you think might have been some of the comforts Jonah had to leave behind in Israel to follow God's instructions?

> If your life is being interrupted right now in some way, what "comforts" are you having the most difficult time leaving behind to follow God's directives?

CHANGING PERSPECTIVE

I wish Jonah could have seen his life laid out in four simple chapters like we can. He would have seen that what he considered an interruption was really an invitation to participate in one of the more supernatural events in all the Old Testament—one that would not only make a mark in the Old but the New Testament as well (Luke 11:30). He couldn't have known that his story would be studied by millions desiring to draw closer to his God.

Yet Jonah probably felt about God's plans the same way you and I often feel—he was frustrated. The importance and priority we've placed on our plans cause us to frown on new assignments the Lord may send our way.

> What other challenges might you face that will make it difficult for you to see life interruptions in a positive way?

Our study of Jonah is primarily about helping us to redefine interruption when it comes to our relationship with God. If He is our priority and His will is our primary purpose, then when the "word of the LORD" comes to us or when He allows us to see His hand in our circumstances, we must see it as an esteemed opportunity to participate in kingdom purposes. What more critical or essential ambition could there be?

So today, my friend, right at the onset of our study, we redefine interruption. God's plan is a "Divine Intervention."

Consider the following equation:

Insignificant Person + Insignificant Task = Interruption

Significant Person + Significant Task = Divine Intervention

Explain the meaning of the equation in your own words.

Interruptions only become positive when we consider the person or the circumstance interrupting to be more significant than that which currently occupies our attention. It is easy to say that God and His plans are our most essential endeavors. It is entirely another thing to live like this is so.

While I love a good in-depth study with deep exploratory questions, I was continually drawn to ask you personal application questions while writing this study. When you turn the last page, you'll no doubt know more about Jonah's story than you may have before, but my primary goal in our time together is to help you dig deeply into its application to your life. Many of the questions I will ask you will focus on how Jonah's story relates to you.

Reworking our view of God and His plans is our goal, particularly this first week. To handle life's interruptions appropriately, the prophet needed a fresh view of God, and over the course of the next few days of his life that is exactly what he was going to get. My prayer is that these seven weeks we spend together will do the same for you and me.

As we place God and His will in a position of significance, I pray that we will be delighted when we hear His voice or see His hand orchestrating our circumstances to align with His purposes.

Conclude today's lesson by listing in the margin your top three aspirations at this point in your life. It could be a goal you have for your children, your career, ministry, finances, or something else. Then take time to meditate on whether you place more importance on them or on God and His purposes for you. Will you yield them to Him if He requests that you do so?

> If you find yourself balking at God's instructions in your life, it is an indication of the importance you place on God and His will.

Day 2

ON THE JOB

"For we are God's fellow workers." 1 Corinthians 3:9

I recently met a young woman who works as a personal assistant to one of the most powerful people in the country. She was delighted when she was offered this coveted job working alongside this highly respected and busy individual. The moment she signed on to be an assistant, she was told that during her working hours she needed to be on call. This meant that at any moment her boss may call her to assist him and she would need to drop anything she was doing—even if she were working on another assignment at the time. While adjusting to fit this schedule was difficult at first, she quickly became used to it and organized her life appropriately.

Now she is constantly waiting on a call from her boss. She makes sure that all of her communication devices are powered up, activated, and just a hand's reach away so that she can be ready to receive instruction. While she does make some personal plans during working hours, she holds them loosely. She is fully aware that her primary responsibility is to be ready to manage that which her boss assigns.

I asked her if she felt overwhelmed or disgusted having to change her personal plans. She shook her head and replied, "No way. It's an honor to have this job. And," she added, "he's a nice guy. While everything he asks for is not always convenient, he's very considerate. I want to do a good job."

When we signed up to follow Christ, we automatically signed up to be open to "Divine Intervention"—God interruptions. While His "call" might not always be convenient or easy, responding to it should not just be a duty but our joy. We are getting the honor of partnering with the Lord in His purposes for this generation. You can count on the promise in Psalm 145:17. He is kind in all of His ways so you don't have to worry that He may take advantage of your loyalty. Partnering with Him doesn't mean having no plans and ambitions of your own. It means holding them loosely, always leaving room for "the word of the LORD" reshaping your purposes and aligning them with His own.

"The LORD is righteous in all His ways and kind in all His deeds."
Psalm 145:17

Rewrite our equations from yesterday's lesson.

Jonah had been a prophet to Israel; now he was being called to Nineveh. (See Jonah 1:2.) Take a moment to find this location on the map in the back of your book and circle it.

Based on Jonah's response, did he consider this a divine intervention or an interruption? Explain.

In the chart below, write how the biblical character was interrupted. Did he see God's instruction as a divine intervention or a negative interruption? Explain.

Name	God's Directive	Interruption or Divine Intervention
Noah	Genesis 6:13-14,17-22	
Gideon	Judges 6:11-27	
Cornelius	Acts 10:1-8	

In the first half of the 8th century B.C., Nineveh was one of the principal provinces in Assyria. The Assyrians had a reputation for inflicting physical and psychological terror on its enemies, including Israel. The Assyrians may have laid siege to Gath-hepher, Jonah's hometown. "Perhaps the city was destroyed and many of the inhabitants slain. Some loved one of Jonah may have suffered and been killed at this time. There is a possibility that his own mother and father were slain before his eyes when he was a boy."[2]

While we can only speculate about details of how Nineveh affected Jonah, Israel definitely had been brutalized by their archenemy. Just the name *Nineveh* would strike bitterness, dread, and fear in the heart of an Israelite. During the 8th century, Assyria was experiencing a time of national weakness and Jonah would have wanted to have seen their decline continue. It would have been his desire to see their complete demise. Yet God was calling Jonah to leave his beloved countrymen and preach to his enemies. Jonah placed no value on Nineveh or on its inhabitants.

I'll never forget a Rwandan couple coming forward for prayer in our church many years ago. They had been evacuated with other survivors during the vast murders of 1994. However, in the rush to leave the country, their children had been left behind. They didn't know if they were alive or dead and could only hope to see them again. The pain in that mother's eyes and the tears falling down the father's face is seared in my memory forever.

Many genocides have taken place in our lifetime. Hundreds of thousands of people have lost their lives at the hands of renegade governments, soldiers, or dictators. While most of us have not been directly affected by this, consider how you might feel if your family suffered at the hands of others and then you were asked to show mercy and concern for them.

Did you grow up with a hatred or fear of any group of people? If so, in the margin note who and why.

God calling Jonah to Nineveh most likely struck the cord of a gut-level, deep-seated hurt with just the mention of the city's name. He had an enormous dislike for this place and its inhabitants.

In our journeys with God, we will likely come across our personal Ninevehs. For some this might actually be a place; for others Nineveh is a task or relationship and just the mention of that mission or person sends us into an emotional tailspin. We'd just rather not go. And, like Jonah, we can point to many reasons that would keep us at home.

Do you have a Nineveh assignment—something God is requiring of you right now that you do not want to do? What are your reasons for not wanting to do it?

MISSIONARY ASSIGNMENT

During the video lesson I encouraged you to start considering how your group can tangibly and practically minister to others during the course of your study. Begin to consider who the Ninevites may be in your world—the unloved, forgotten, seemingly unreachable ones.

PRIVILEGED TO BE INTERRUPTED

God graciously gives divine interventions to His children. He presents them an opportunity to partner with Him in purposes they could never conceive. A life interrupted by a holy God is a privilege. Believers must internalize this principle in order to live a life that accomplishes God's will.

God doesn't need us to complete His purposes, yet He still chooses to ask us to partner with Him. It's unfathomable. His calling you means that He has chosen you above anyone else to do what He is asking. You are the one He singled out and pinpointed as His partner for a particular project.

Whether it's parenting a special needs child, starting a Bible study, remaining single for a bit longer, or even, like Jonah, reaching out to those who hurt you, He's purposefully given you the high honor of being the one He deemed suited for a task that has heavenly implications—a task of divine partnership that will yield magnificent results for you and for His kingdom. While these benefits might not be visible at the outset, a supernatural outcome waits on the horizon for anyone who chooses to partner with God.

> For each of the biblical characters you just studied, how did each culminate in unimaginable results?
>
> Noah (Gen. 8:18-22)
>
> Gideon (Judg. 8:22)
>
> Cornelius (Acts 10:30-48)
>
>
> From the following verses, list the ways Jonah's life became one of eternal significance:
>
> Jonah 3:4-5
>
> Luke 11:30

God's calling you means He has chosen you above anyone else.

Believing that divine interruptions are a privilege not only will cause us to handle them differently but also to await them eagerly. Knowing that we have an opportunity to participate in God's purposes should cause us to sit on the edge of our seats in anticipation of divine interventions disguised as life's interruptions.

SIGNIFICANTLY YOU

We know very little about Jonah. In fact, until the four chapters of this book, his life seems fairly insignificant. Jonah is a lone character with one known relative: his father. His dad's name and his birthplace are only mentioned twice in the entirety of Scripture. No other record of his lineage

17

exists. Everything we know about the prophet before the Book of Jonah shows up in 2 Kings 14:25. Pay special attention to it now.

Record Jonah's "résumé" from 2 Kings.

His name:

His hometown:

His religion:

His job:

His closest relative:

These five details about Jonah sum up what we know about him. Nothing is particularly noteworthy. Not until he received a divine interruption did he develop a life story that made a stamp on history. The bulk of what Scripture teaches about this prophet and certainly the most eternally significant part of this man's life comes after God interrupted.

When Jonah heard a word from God—and finally yielded to it—his ordinary existence became extraordinary. Not only did Jonah spark the greatest revival in all human history but as a result of his mission he was mentioned in the New Testament by Jesus. Jonah's true significance began with a divine intervention.

Divine Intervention + Yielded Submission = ETERNAL SIGNIFICANCE

Rewrite this equation in your own words below.

When God chose Jonah to go to Nineveh, it was a privilege. His story began when he yielded to God's divine intervention, and it made an eternal imprint on humanity. Whatever God has called you to do should be a privilege for you to undertake. While it might not be easy or convenient, He offers you a chance to write a story of significance for eternity.

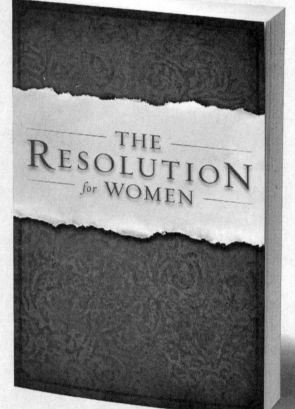